Living LITERATURE

LINKING TEXTS

Jackie Baker

Hodder & Stoughton

A MEMBER OF THE HODDER HEADLINE GROUP

Acknowledgements

The publishers would like to thank the following for their kind permission to reproduce copyright material:

p.6 *Warning* by Jenny Joseph, reproduced by permission of the author; care of John Johnson Ltd., 1986; *On Ageing* from The Complete Collected Poems by Maya Angelou, Virago Press, 1994; p.11 *Sunny Prestatyn* by Philip Larkin, Longman Group, 1979; p.12 *Aubade* by Philip Larkin, Faber & Faber, 1988; p.16 extract from *Cider with Rosie* by Laurie Lee, published by Hogarth Press. Used by permission of The Random House Group Limited; p.23 *Suicide in the Trenches* by Siegfred Sassoon, Faber & Faber, 1990; p.24 *The Suicide* by Louis MacNiece, reproduced by permission of the author; care of David Higham Associated; p.31 *I Know Why the Caged Bird Sings* by Maya Angelou, Little, Brown and Company, 1984; p.33 *Oleander, Jacaranda: A Childhood Perceived* by Penelope Lively (Viking, 1994) © Penelope Lively, 1994; p.38 Taken from the back cover of *Notes From A Small Island* by Bill Bryson, first published by Transworld Publishers, a division of the Random House Group, in 1995. All rights reserved.; p.39 *The Kingdom By The Sea* by Paul Theroux, Washington Square Press, 1983; p.39 *Broke Through Britain* by Peter Mortimer, Mainstream Publishing, 1999; p.40 *Home Truths* by Bill Murphy, Mainstream Publishing, 2000; p.42 *Notes From A Small Island* by Bill Bryson, first published by Transworld Publishers, a division of the Random House Group, in 1995. All rights reserved.; p.42 *At Grass* by Philip Larkin, The Marvell Press, 1968; p.45 *The Horses* by Edwin Muir, from *Poetry 1900–1975*, reproduced by permission of Faber & Faber; p.47 Ian Smythe's cover illustration, *Robinson Crusoe* by Daniel Defoe, Everyman, by kind permission of J.M Dent; Paul Hogarth's cover illustration, *The Lord of the Flies* by William Golding, reproduced by permission of Faber & Faber, 1954; cover illustration, *The Beach* by Alex Garland, Penguin, 1996; p.51 *Things Fall Apart* by Chinua Achebe, Heinemann, 1958; p.52 *The Royal Hunt of the Sun* by Peter Shaffer, Longman, 1966; p.53 *1984* by George Orwell, Penguin, 1948; p.53 extract from *The Handmaid's Tale* by Margaret Atwood, published by Jonathan Cape. Used by permission of the Random House Group Ltd., 1987; p.55 *Long Distance* by Tony Harrison, from *Selected Poems*, Penguin © Tony Harrison, 1985; p.55 *Dad* by Elaine Feinstein, Bloodaxe, 1985; p.57 *Old Ladies Home* by Sylvia Plath, used by permission of Faber & Faber, 1981; p.57 *Two Black Men on a Leicester Square Park Bench* from *The Fat Black Woman's Poems* by Grace Nichols, Little, Brown and Company; p.58 *A Difficult Child* by Zulfikar Ghose, Macmillan; p.58 *The Good Teachers* is taken from *Mean Time* by Carol Ann Duffy, published by Anvil Press, 1993; p.59 *The Wife's Tale* by Seamus Heaney, Faber & Faber, 1966; p.60 *Portrait of A Marriage* by Dannie Abse, © Danny Abse, from *Collected Poems 1948–88 White Coat, Purple Coat*, Hutchinson, 1989; p.62 *The Nurse of the Man in the Pink Pyjamas* and *Noun Phrases* by Jeremy Hughes, © Jeremy Hughes 2000; p.65 *The Battlefield* by Emily Dickinson, Longman, 1994; p.65 *Jeux d'Enfants* by S. Russell Jones, University Tutorial Press, 1983; p.66 *My Family* by Paul D. Wapshott © Paul D. Wapshott, BBC Enterprises Ltd, Longman, 1989; p.67 *The Letter* by Wilfred Owen, p.67 *What Were They Like* by Denise Levertov © Levertov, BBC Enterprises Ltd., Longman, 1989; p.68 *Air Raid* by Charles Robinson © Robinson, BBC Enterprises and Longman, 1989; p.68 *Your Attention Please* by Peter Porter © Porter, BBC Enterprises and Longman, 1989; p.69 *The Identification* by Roger McGough, Reprinted by permission of PFD on behalf of Roger McGough © Roger McGough, as printed in the original volume, 1989; p.72 *Marriage* by Elaine Feinstein, Bloodaxe, 1985; p.76 *Bed Among the Lentils* by Alan Bennett from *Talking Heads*, BBC, 1988; p.77 extracts from Penguin Book of Modern Women's Short Stories, ed. Susan Hill, Penguin, 1990; p.77 *The Weekend* by Fay Weldon, Penguin, 1990; p.80 *Toads* by Philip Larkin, The Marvell Press. 1977; p.87 *The Fatal Shore* by Robert Hughes © Robert Hughes, 1986 Reproduced by permission of The Harvill Press.; p.87 *The Playmaker* by Thomes Keneally, Serpentine Publishing, 1987; p.90 *Down Under* by Bill Bryson, Doubleday, 2000; p.91 *The Beach* by Alex Garland, Penguin, 1996; p.91 *Lord of the Flies* by William Golding, Faber & Faber, 1954; p.93 *Blackberry Picking* from *New Selected Poems 1966–1987* by Seamus Heaney, Faber & Faber, 1987; p.93 *The Burning of Leaves* by Lawernce Binyon, Penguin, 1962; p.98 *The Remains of the Day* by Kazuo Ishiguro, Faber & Faber, 1989; p.98 *Talking It Over* by Julian Barnes, Picador, 1991; p.99 *As I Lay Dying* by William Faulkner, © Faulkner 1930; p.100 *Last Orders* by Graham Swift, Macmillan, London UK, 1996; p.102 *Death of A Naturalist* by Seamus Heaney, Faber & Faber, 1980; p.103 *Christmas Shopping* by Louis MacNiece, reproduced by permission of the author, care of David Highan Associated, 1997.

Every effort has been made to trace copyright holders of materials reproduced in this book. Any rights not acknowledged will be acknowledged in subsequent printings if notice is given to the publisher.

Orders: please contact Bookpoint Ltd, 130 Milton Park, Abingdon, Oxon OX14 4SB. Telephone: (44) 01235 827720, Fax: (44) 01235 400454. Lines are open from 9.00 - 6.00, Monday to Saturday, with a 24 hour message answering service. Email address: orders@bookpoint.co.uk

British Library Cataloguing in Publication Data
A catalogue record for this title is available from The British Library

ISBN 0 340 79952 8

First published 2001
Impression number   10 9 8 7 6 5 4 3 2 1
Year   2007 2006 2005 2004 2003 2002 2001

Copyright © 2001 Jackie Baker

Cover photo © Ray Export Company Establishment
Typeset by Fakenham Photosetting Limited, Fakenham, Norfolk
Printed in Great Britain for Hodder & Stoughton Educational, a division of Hodder Headline Plc, 338 Euston Road, London NW1 3BH by J.W. Arrowsmith Ltd, Bristol.

Contents

Thanks to staff and students of Itchen College, Southampton, in particular Joan Cawte for writing a comparative essay!

Thanks to Emma Cook for additional material.

Thanks to Richard Baker for practical and moral support.

Thanks to Julian, Amanda, Sonia, and Nicholas for always showing an interest!

1 What's it all About?

In this opening chapter we shall be exploring the whole concept of what linking texts is all about and how to do it successfully. We shall be looking at particular areas which may form the beginning of a comparison. We shall look at specific texts to demonstrate ideas. It may be that you have not read many of these texts but you should be able to learn some techniques and pick up some ideas whether you know these texts or not. This chapter aims to highlight significant areas and get you thinking and studying in preparation for tasks that require you to explore the relationship between two texts. More detailed strategies are suggested in the succeeding chapters.

You will have to develop your skills in this area for your full A Level qualification no matter which subject specifications you are following. The main Assessment Objective covered in this book is AO2ii and this is tested, as you know, either in coursework or in examination. This AO is tested at A Level only and requires that you 'respond with knowledge and understanding to literary texts of different types and periods, exploring and commenting on relationships and comparisons between literary texts'. You may have a free choice of texts or you may have a specific text or texts chosen for you. You may have to look at whole texts that were written in different periods (defined as having been written at least thirty years apart). There may be regulations regarding genre (the type or form of the texts) and the cultural milieu (the time and context in which the texts were written). You may have to choose a particular literary topic area, for example the Victorian novel, twentieth century American literature or humorous writing.

Whatever method you are assessed by and whatever restrictions you are faced with, you have to show knowledge and understanding of literary texts from different times and of different genres and 'explore and comment on relationships and comparisons' between them.

In your study of literature so far you have probably studied a book, put your copy of the text and notes away for a while, and then gone on to study another text. What you have to do now is keep one text in your mind and consider another one and its possible relationship to the first. This becomes surprisingly rewarding – even addictive – as you begin to consider all the possible similarities and differences between texts. Each text becomes more interesting as you delve deeper into its relationship to another.

Let's dip into a few ideas to set you thinking.

What does linking mean?

ACTIVITY 1

Link, connect, compare, contrast, distinguish, differentiate, join, attach, pair, combine, intertwine, unite . . . Can you think of any other synonyms?

Using these synonyms you can produce a chart which shows that links can be in the form of differences as well as similarities. Add your own suggestions to the chart below.

Similarities	Differences
link	contrast
connect	distinguish
compare	differentiate
join	
attach	
pair	
combine	
intertwine	
unite	

Resemblances

Are you tired of people saying, 'Don't you look like your Dad!'? It is only second in tediousness to the comment, 'Well, aren't you growing up!' Linking texts is a little like noticing family resemblances. When you first meet a family you may see superficial resemblances very clearly. You may not be able to distinguish between siblings and distinguishing between twins seems impossible. However, as you get to know a family more intimately you see that they are in fact very different and after a while you may fail to see any resemblance at all. Subtle *differences* become obvious. This is what happens when you look at two texts that are linked in some way. When you become more familiar with them you begin to notice all sorts of differences. However, you will always be aware that the family members all originally came from the same 'stock'. In the case of texts they may come from the same genre, may have the same theme, or be written in the same time or culture, or by the same author and this will account for the similarities. These perspectives will be examined in this book. The differences are, of course, the result of the flair and originality of the writer.

ACTIVITY 2

A bit of fun

Find two books that have a character called Ralph.

Find two books that have a character called Jane.

Find two books that are set in the same place.

Take two texts that have no similarities at all at first glance and find some.

This may or may not be a productive way of selecting books to compare but it will set you thinking about where to start. It will also test your ingenuity!

Famous families

You may think that books by the same author or members of the same family would be a good start to thinking about choosing linking texts. This may well be so but it's not as easy as you may think.

You will already be aware of some famous families. The Fonda family are all famous actors, as are Michael Douglas and his father Kirk. The brothers Julian and Andrew Lloyd Webber are famous musicians but in quite different fields. The Dimbleby brothers followed their famous father into broadcasting.

Martin and Kingsley Amis are famous father and son writers. The Brontë sisters and their brother are another example. The obvious connection is the family name but the resemblance may or may not go beyond that.

ACTIVITY 3

Shall I compare thee ...?

1 Find out what you can about Kingsley and Martin Amis and the type of writing they are famous for. You could try looking on the Internet, in books about the modern British novel or even at some of the novels they wrote. Developing your own research skills is something you should try to do throughout your A-level course.
As they are father and son their writing is a

generation apart. Notice they are both satirical writers and also both wrote in different genres.

2 Do the same for the Brontës. Remember that there were three sisters and a brother and they wrote poetry as well as novels. Perhaps the easiest approach is through the idea that many of the stories and characters are autobiographical.

COMMENTARY   The Brontës were reared together and had access to the same books when they were children. They encouraged each other to write fiction from an early age creating the fictional worlds of Gondal and Angria. The sisters all were governesses at some point and women with this profession feature in many of their novels. Branwell's dissolute behaviour is the model for a character in Anne's second novel *The Tenant of Wildfell Hall*. The cruel Lowood School in *Jane Eyre* is based on the school attended by two of the sisters. The novels are surprisingly intense for the daughters of a clergyman and they are mysterious as well as insular and parochial. It is interesting to note that at one point Charlotte and Anne visited their publishers together to prove that there were two different authors at work! Their novels were considered as almost inappropriate for young women to read and an unlikely product of their sheltered environment. Today the novels of these sisters are considered to be among the most important of the nineteenth century and make fascinating reading.

Branwell's 'gun group' portrait

From your research you may feel that a comparative study of the role of women in their novels would be productive or a study of the social conditions of the time or a study of the different narrative techniques used. You could also study the creation of place and character. Any of these suggestions would be a fruitful area of study.

Same word processor – different printout!

You may think that comparing two books by the same author would be profitable. It may be very interesting but may not prove to be enough for a really in-depth response. It may be interesting to look at one author writing in a different genre.

For example, Maya Angelou wrote poetry as well as her autobiography in several volumes. (You might like to look up *On the Pulse of Morning* which she wrote for and read at the inauguration of President Clinton in 1993 and compare it to the ideas expressed in the first volume of her autobiography *I Know Why the Caged Bird Sings*.) Another of her poems, *On Ageing*, is printed later in this chapter and you could compare its tone and language with that of her autobiography.

ACTIVITY 4

Random reactions

1 Pluck out of your head, or your bookcase, two texts. With a bit of luck they will appear to be wildly different – unless your bookcase is more organised than most!
Try to assemble a list of similarities. Here are some possibilities:

- same length
- same publisher
- same author
- same genre
- same point of view
- same location
- characters with the same or similar names
- same number of chapters
- same general subject matter
- same structure e.g. chronological or not
- same time e.g. present day or set in earlier times
- same purpose
- same theme.

2 When you have sorted out some similarities, decide which ones are actually significant and rank them in order of importance.
Alternatively you could use the list above and rank these similarities in order of importance without referring to particular texts.

3 Now deliberately choose two books that seem very similar and work out what the *differences* are. Are the books really worth comparing or linking?

By now you will be gaining in confidence and using the skills and knowledge you already have. You are probably also thinking that the whole process is more involved than at first seemed to be the case. That is why you must think, research and examine the texts very carefully before you make your final choice.

Getting down to it – the nitty gritty

The chapters which follow will give you more information, strategies and ideas about how to go about making some links. Here we shall continue to examine some general principles which will be useful.

To link or not to link ...

Author, time, genre, theme, style, characters, location, structure, method of narration ... the list of areas to consider is quite long and this one is not exhaustive. It is likely that one or two of these topics will form the major part of the comparison but nearly all of these aspects will be relevant and productive. Although, in this book, the perspectives have been separated you should consider as many of these perspectives as you can when developing your essay in order to show a really significant and thorough response.

As a general strategy it is a good idea to base your comparison on texts that have at least two basic similarities. The diagram which follows should be helpful in establishing this idea. The lines connecting the circles indicate the main similarities and the lines off each circle indicate the main differences. You could begin your investigation by drawing and labelling a diagram like this one for two texts that you know well.

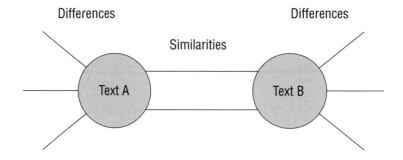

1 Here are two poems on how to deal with getting old. Using the idea of the chart given above, begin to decide on the areas of similarity and difference in these two poems.

Now draw a chart to help you firm up your ideas. You may need to adjust the number of connections and the number of unconnected arms!

Warning

When I am an old woman I shall wear purple
With a red hat which doesn't go, and doesn't suit me.
And I shall spend my pension on brandy and summer gloves
And satin sandals, and say we've no money for butter.
I shall sit down on the pavement when I'm tired
And gobble up samples in shops and press alarm bells
And run my stick along the public railings
And make up for the sobriety of my youth.
I shall go out in my slippers in the rain
And pick the flowers in other people's gardens
And learn to spit.

You can wear terrible skirts and grow more fat
And eat three pounds of sausages at a go
Or only bread and pickle for week
And hoard pens and pencils and beer mats and things in boxes.

But now we must have clothes that keep us dry
And pay our rent and not swear in the street
And set a good example for the children.
We must have friends to dinner and read the papers.

But maybe I ought to practise a little now?
So people who know me are not too shocked and surprised
When suddenly I am old, and start to wear purple.

Jenny Joseph

On Ageing

When you see me sitting quietly,
Like a sack left on the shelf,
Don't think I need your chattering,
I'm listening to myself.

Hold! Stop! Don't pity me!
Hold! Stop your sympathy!
Understanding if you got it,
Otherwise I'll do without it!

When my bones are stiff and aching
And my feet won't climb the stairs,
I will only ask one favour:
Don't bring me no rocking chair.

When you see me walking, stumbling,
Don't study and get it wrong.
'Cause tired don't mean lazy
And every goodbye ain't gone.

I'm the same person I was back then,
A little less hair, a little less chin,
A lot less lungs and much less wind,
But ain't I lucky I can still breathe in.

Maya Angelou

You may have come up with some of the following ideas.
Connections:

- Theme of ageing
- Both are women writers
- Rebellious/aggressive ideas
- Non-standard diction.

Differences:

- Joseph's poem stresses what she wants to do/Angelou's poems stresses how she wants to be treated
- Angelou's poem uses black English/Joseph's is simply colloquial

- Joseph's poem reads from the point of view of a middle class woman
- Joseph's poem is looking to the future/Angelou's poem is in the present
- The tone of the Angelou poem is aggressive towards the listener/Joseph's is more contemplative.

2 Now that you have worked through these two poems about ageing, you should be in a position to write a detailed comparison between them. Have a go!

Genre, theme, style and structure are dealt with elsewhere. In this introductory chapter, comparisons based on author, cultural/historical milieu, characters and location will be examined.

Same author – spot the difference if you can!

You can do a careful comparison of two works by the same author. You could do this by looking at the portrayal of major characters or the development of significant themes. Jane Austen's heroines or Charles Dickens' comic characters would be good starting points. You could look at the difference between early and late work by an author or works in different genres. For example, Thomas Hardy was a poet as well as a novelist. You might find it interesting to look at the historical context of the texts and the effect of incidents in the life of the writer. There is a great deal to consider! However, similarities will be easier to spot than differences, especially if you look in detail at the writer's style.

ACTIVITY 6

1 Here are the opening paragraphs of two novels by Thomas Hardy. Look at them carefully and decide if you would have been able to deduce that they were written by the same author.

2 Write down what you learn about the appearance of each character and suggest what you learn about the nature of the person described.

3 Study and make a comment on the sentence structure the writer uses.

4 Comment on any words that you think are unusual or significant. Find out if they are dialect or just 'old fashioned'.

5 Comment on the use of figurative language.

There will be more help with this in a later chapter but you probably already have a lot of good ideas and knowledge to start this process even at this stage.

The Mayor of Casterbridge

One evening of late summer, before the nineteenth century had reached one third of its span, a young man and woman, the latter carrying a child, were approaching the large village of Weydon-Priors, in upper Wessex on foot. They were plainly but not ill clad, though the thick hoar of dust which had accumulated on their shoes and garments from an obviously long journey lent a disadvantageous shabbiness to their appearance just now.

The man was of fine figure, swarthy, and stern in aspect; and he showed in profile a facial angle so slightly inclined as to be almost perpendicular. He wore a short jacket of brown corduroy, newer than the remainder of his suit, which was a fustian waistcoat with white horn buttons, breeches of the same, tanned leggings, and a straw hat overlaid with black glazed canvas. At his back he carried by a looped strap a rush basket from which protruded at one end the crutch of a hay-knife, a wimble for hay-bonds being also visible in the aperture. His measured springless walk was the walk of the skilled countryman as distinct from the desultory shamble of the general labourer; while in the turn and plant of each foot there was, further, a dogged and cynical indifference, personal to himself, showing its presence even in the regularly interchanging fustian folds, now in the left leg, now in the right, as he paced along.

Far from the Madding Crowd

Since he lived six times as many working days as Sundays, Oak's appearance was most peculiarly his own – the mental picture formed by his neighbours in imagining him being dressed in that way. He wore a low-formed felt hat, spread out at the base by tight jamming upon his head for security in high winds, and a coat like Dr Johnson's; his lower extremities being encased in ordinary leather leggings and boots emphatically large, affording to each foot a roomy compartment so constructed that any wearer might stand in a river all day long and know nothing of damp – their maker being a conscientious man who endeavoured to compensate for any weakness in his cut by unstinted dimension and solidity.

Mr Oak carried about him by way of watch, what may be called a small silver clock; in other words, it was a watch as to shape and intention, and a small clock as to size. This instrument, being several years older than Oak's grandfather, had the peculiarity of going either too fast or not at all. The smaller of its hands, too, occasionally slipped round on the pivot, and thus, though the minutes were told with precision, nobody could be quite certain of the hour they belonged to. The stopping peculiarity of his watch Oak remedied by thumps and shakes, and he escaped any evil consequences from the other two defects by constant comparisons with and observations of the sun and stars, and by pressing his face close to the glass of his neighbours' windows, till he could discern the hour marked by green-faced time keepers within. It may be mentioned that Oak's fob being difficult of access, by reason of its somewhat high situation in the waistband of his trousers (which also lay at a remote height under his waistcoat), the watch was as a necessity pulled out by throwing the body to one side, compressing the mouth and face to a mere mass of ruddy flesh on account of the exertion, and drawing up the watch by its chain, like a bucket from a well.

COMMENTARY These extracts come from the early part of the novels. Hardy is intent on establishing the reality of his characters by giving the reader as much detail as possible about their appearance and actions.

There is detail of the headgear of the characters and also the rest of their clothes. Hardy tells us in detail what each is carrying and also describes significant actions. Hardy's sentences are long and involved and his language often circuitous (that is, he does not write concisely!). So far so good but what else is there? Hardy's lexis (vocabulary) is somewhat different from ours. 'Hoar of dust', 'clad', 'wimble', 'aperture', 'fustian' are words from the first extract with which you may not be familiar. 'Low-formed' to describe a hat is rather unusual. Do we really know what sort of coat Dr Johnson would have worn? When did you last use the word 'fob'? There is only one use of figurative language in these extracts and that is Hardy's description of Oak's action when he retrieves his watch from his trousers as 'like a bucket from a well'.

So it is fairly easy and obvious to see similarities in the style of different texts by the same author. The way forward would be perhaps to choose an early and a late novel or concentrate more on the themes and issues featured in the texts rather than the style.

The delicateness of Jane Austen

ACTIVITY 7

Here is an extract from the beginning of *Pride and Prejudice*. It shows Jane Austen's shrewd observation of human nature.

Pick out the modifiers (describing words) used to describe Bingley and Darcy. What causes the change in attitude of the company?

What is Jane Austen saying about human nature here? How would you describe the tone?

Mr Bingley was good-looking and gentlemanlike; he had a pleasant countenance, and easy, unaffected manners. His sisters were fine women, with an air of decided fashion. His brother-in-law, Mr Hurst, merely looked the gentleman; but his friend Mr Darcy soon drew the attention of the room by his fine, tall person, handsome features, noble mien – and the report which was in general circulation within five minutes after his entrance of his having ten thousand a year. The gentlemen pronounced him to be a fine figure of a man, the ladies declared he was much handsomer than Mr Bingley, and he was looked at with great admiration for about half the evening, till his manners gave a disgust which turned the tide of his popularity; for he was discovered to be proud, to be above his company, and above being pleased; and not all his large estate in Derbyshire could then save him from having a most forbidding, disagreeable countenance, and being unworthy to be compared to his friend.

COMMENTARY Jane Austen cannot be bettered for her gentle castigation of social foibles.

The modifiers used for Bingley are 'good-looking', 'gentlemanlike', 'pleasant', 'easy', 'unaffected'. Darcy is at first 'fine', 'tall', 'handsome', 'noble', but when he fails to respond to their delightful company he becomes 'proud', 'forbidding', 'disagreeable', 'unworthy'. It is when he is rumoured to be richer than Bingley that he becomes the more handsome of the two and when he insults the company with his supposed pride that he becomes less handsome! Money seems to dictate handsomeness and seeming bad manners detract immediately from physical appearance. Jane Austen is well aware of subjective opinions which are given the status of fact.

Glance through another novel by Jane Austen and find another passage which echoes this subtle criticism of social prejudice. The first paragraph of *Mansfield Park* and the beginning of *Emma* are good places to start.

So, you can look at two different passages by the same author but the comparison is difficult and limited. Similarities will abound but you may struggle to find differences which are fruitful. You may be lucky in finding two texts that have a great deal to write about but then again . . .

Poets with attitude

The poets John Donne and Philip Larkin are separated by approximately three hundred and fifty years. However, in tone and style there are many similarities. These poets both challenged their readers and tried to shock. They are not alone in this aim. Many authors, in particular poets, have this desire to shock! Can you think of any other poets whose style and subject matter could be seen as offensive? You could look at some of the poems of the contemporary poet, Tony Harrison, or, if you think you are unshockable, at the Restoration poet, the Earl of Rochester. But you should be able to think of some examples for yourself.

ACTIVITY 8

1 Study this poem by Larkin. Pick out anything that you think might be offensive or any words or phrases that it is surprising to find in poetry.

Sunny Prestatyn

Come to sunny Prestatyn
Laughed the girl on the poster,
Kneeling up on the sand
In tautened white satin.
Behind her, a hunk of coast, a
Hotel with palms
Seemed to expand from her thighs and
Spread breast lifting arms.

She was slapped up one day in March.
A couple of weeks, and her face
Was snaggle-toothed and boss-eyed;
Huge tits and a fissured crotch
Were scored well in, and the space
Between her legs held scrawls
That set her fairly astride
A tuberous cock and balls

Autographed *Titch Thomas*, while
Someone had used a knife
Or something to stab right through
The moustached lips of her smile.
She was too good for this life.
Very soon, a great transverse tear
Left only a hand and a bit of blue.
Now *Fight Cancer* is there.

Philip Larkin

Obviously there is something brutal about this poem but it has a serious purpose. Perhaps it is about violence and destruction as well as the real concerns of human pain and the subversion of pleasant images by people who resent them. The poem begins with a pleasant image of a holiday destination but by the second stanza the subversion begins. The girl was 'slapped up' and her features distorted by knives and pens. She was stabbed and 'scored' by a knife. The laughing girl is made to have 'snaggle' teeth and 'boss' eyes. The unpleasant and offensive 'tuberous cock and balls' distort the pleasant holiday image. Her breasts and thighs are referred to with the crude expressions: 'huge tits' and 'fissured crotch'. The ideal was too good, too unreal and is destroyed and replaced by the reality of cancer.

2 Now look at this poem by John Donne. Although Donne's poetry varies from the religious to the profane he still has the ability to shock his readers. In one of his 'divine poems' he refers directly to his misspent youth.

Holy Sonnet III

O might those sighes and teares returne againe
Into my breast and eyes, which I have spent,
That I might in this holy discontent
Mourne with some fruit, as I have mourned in vaine;
In mine Idolatry what showres of raine

Mine eyes did waste? What griefs my heart did rent?
That sufferance was my sinne I now repent,
'Cause I did suffer I must suffer paine.
Th' hydroptic drunkard, and night scouring thiefe,
The itchy Lecher, and selfe tickling proud
Have the remembrance of past joyes, for reliefe
Of coming ills. To (poore) me is allowed
No ease; for, long, yet vehement griefe hath beene
Th' effect and cause, the punishment and sinne.

John Donne

In this poem he is attempting to weep for his sins in the same way as he wept in the 'idolatry' of his youth. His earlier tears were wasted and he should not have spent his grief on such triviality. He is paying for this now by not being able to 'mourne with some fruit'. He feels that thieves and drunkards and 'the itchy lecher' are better off than he is. The idolatry of his youth is juxtaposed with his present 'holy discontent'.

Some of the poetry of Donne centres around death and funerals with graphic details of burials and autopsies. Larkin's poetry is often an attack on contemporary beliefs and behaviour. Both try to shock their readers and use language that is on the brink of unacceptable. They also write about some taboo subjects.

ACTIVITY 9

Here are two more poems by these poets. Both are set in a bedroom and have the urgency and directness which we associate with these poets.

Establish the theme and tone of each poem.

Examine the language to uncover the individuality and also the similarity of style and tone.

Aubade

I work all day, and get half drunk at night.
Waking at four to soundless dark, I stare.
In time the curtain edges will grow light.
Till then I see what's really always there:
Unresting death, a whole day nearer now,
Making all thought impossible but how
And where and when I shall myself die.
Arid interrogation: yet the dread
Of dying, and being dead,
Flashes afresh to hold and horrify.

The mind blanks at the glare. Not in remorse –
The good not used, the love not given, time
Torn off unused – nor wretchedly because
An only life can take so long to climb
Clear of its wrong beginnings, and may never:
But at the total emptiness forever,
The sure extinction that we travel to
And shall be lost in always. Not to be here,
Not to be anywhere,
And soon; nothing more terrible, nothing more true.

This is a special way of being afraid
No trick dispels. Religion used to try,
That vast moth-eaten musical brocade
Created to pretend we never die,
And specious stuff that says No rational being
Can fear a thing it cannot feel, not seeing
That this is what we fear – no sight, no sound,
No touch or taste or smell, nothing to think with,
Nothing to love or link with,
The anaesthetic from which none come round
And so it stays just on the edge of vision,
A small unfocused blur, a standing chill
That slows most impulses down to indecision.
Most things may never happen: this one will.
And realisation of it rages out
In furnace fear when we are caught without
People or drink. Courage is no good:
It means not scaring others. Being brave
Lets no-one off the grave.
Death is no different whined at than withstood.

Slowly light strengthens, and the room takes shape.

It stands plain as a wardrobe, what we know,
Have always known, know that we can't escape
Yet can't accept. One side will have to go.
Meanwhile telephones crouch, getting ready to ring

In locked up offices, and all the uncaring
Intricate rented world begins to rouse.
The sky is white as clay, with no sun.
Work has to be done.
Postmen like doctors go from house to house.

Philip Larkin

The Sunne Rising

Busie old foole, unruly Sunne,
Why dost thou thus,
Through windowes, and through curtaines call on us?
Must to thy motions lovers seasons run?
Sawcy pedantique wretch, goe chide
Late schoole boyes and sowre prentices,
Goe tell Court-huntsmen, that the King will ride,
Call countrey ants to harvest offices;
Love, all alike, no season knowes, nor clyme,
Nor houres, nor days, moneths which are the rags of time.

Thy beames, so reverend, and strong
Why shouldst thou think?
I could eclipse and cloud them with a winke,
But that I would not lose her sight so long:
If her eyes have not blinded thine,

Looke, and to morrow late, tell mee,
Whether both th' India's of spice and Myne
Be where thou left them, or lie here with mee.
Aske for those Kings whom thou saw'st yesterday,
And thou shalt heare, All here in one bed lay.

She's all States, and all Princes, I,
Nothing else is.
Princes do but play us, compar'd to this,
All honor's mimique: All wealth alchimie;
Thou sunne art halfe as happy as wee,
In that world's contracted thus.
Thine age askes ease, and since thy duties be
To warme the world, that's done in warming us.
Shine here to us, and thou are everywhere;
This bed thy centre is, these walls thy spheare.

John Donne

Looking for links

Authors can be linked in many ways. Here are some suggestions:

- ethnic origin
- gender
- age/era when they were writing
- experiences (e.g. poverty, persecution)
- beliefs (e.g. religious or philosophical)

Can you think of any other ways?

Alice Walker and Maya Angelou can be linked for many of these reasons. You could find out about *I Know Why the Caged Bird Sings* and *The Color Purple* and see how they both tackle the issues that concern them. Remember that you can find information about writers and their works in a good encyclopaedia, a literary history or on the Internet.

Link: Cultural/Historical Milieu

Charles Dickens (1812–1870) and George Eliot (1819–1880) were contemporaries. However, there is surprisingly little reference to political events of the time in their writing. Both novelists set their novels against the same social background. Both resent the poverty associated with people leaving the land for the towns. Both include characters from a wide variety of social backgrounds in their writing.

The Brontë sisters were almost contemporaries of George Eliot. These women published their work under the names of men but only George Eliot's pseudonym has been retained. What does the use of male names tell you about the social climate for writers in the middle of the nineteenth century?

There is more discussion on the cultural milieu of texts in Chapter 4.

Link: Famous villains, famous lovers, famous fathers, famous heroines

As well as attitude and purposes, authors can also be linked by the types of characters they depict.

ACTIVITY 10

Villains, lovers, fathers, heroines. Divide your group into four and spend some time researching one of these categories in each group. Find a description of a famous literary villain, lover and so on and find some suitable quotations to demonstrate the writers' skill. Villains may include several by Shakespeare for example Edmund (*King Lear*), Iago (*Othello*), Angelo (*Measure for Measure*) or some by Dickens for example Uriah Heep (*David Copperfield*), Orlick (*Great Expectations*). What about Mr Darcy (*Pride and Prejudice*), Paul Morel (*Sons and Lovers*) and Mr Knightley (*Emma*) for lovers? When you pool your information you should be able to formulate some ideas about figures in literature and how they are created by different authors.

Link: Locations

You could link texts by the locations that the authors describe. For example there are many famous schools, such as Dotheboys Hall in Dickens' *Nicholas Nickleby* or Llanabba Castle in Evelyn Waugh's comic novel, *Decline and Fall*.

ACTIVITY 11

Study this delightful description of his early days at school by Laurie Lee in *Cider with Rosie*.

1 Pick out the appeals to the senses. Look for sight, sound, touch etc. Decide what the tone of the piece is. Tone is the attitude of the writer to the subject matter and/or the reader. Words to describe tone include *amused, angry, mocking, critical, aggressive, reflective* and so on.

2 Pick out the simple similes.

3 Look for unsophisticated childlike language and also the more reflective and sophisticated language of the writer.

4 Notice the effect of the use of the first person – that is 'I' – as the method of narration. Much of the interest in this extract is created by the immediacy of the use of the first person.

This passage will be referred to again in the chapter on stylistic comparison.

The village school at that time provided all the instruction we were likely to ask for. It was a small stone barn divided by a wooden partition into two rooms – The Infants and The Big Ones. There was one dame teacher, and perhaps a young girl assistant. Every child in the valley crowding there, remained till he was fourteen years old, then was presented to the working field or factory with nothing in his head more burdensome than a few mnemonics, a jumbled list of wars, and a dreamy image of the world's geography. It seemed enough to get by with, in any case; and was one up on our poor old grandparents.

This school, when I came to it, was at its peak. Universal education and unusual fertility had packed it to the walls with pupils. Wild boys and girls from miles around – from the outlying farms and half-hidden hovels way up at the end of the valley – swept down each day to add to our numbers, and bringing with them strange oaths and odours, quaint garments and curious pies. They were my first amazed vision of any world outside the womanly warmth of my family; I didn't expect to survive it for long, and I was confronted with it at the age of four.

The morning came, without any warning, when my sisters surrounded me, wrapped me in scarves, tied up my bootlaces, thrust a cap on my head, and stuffed a baked potato in my pocket.
  'What's this?' I said.
  'You're starting school today.'
  'I ain't. I'm stopping 'ome.'
  'Now, come on, Lol. You're a big boy now.'
  'I ain't'.
  'You are.'
  'Boo-hoo.'
  They picked me up bodily, kicking and bawling, and carried me up the road.
  'Boys who don't go to school get put into boxes, and turned into rabbits, and get chopped up on Sundays.'
  I felt this was overdoing it rather, but I said no more after that. I arrived at school just three feet tall and fatly wrapped in my scarves. The playground roared like a rodeo, and the potato burned through my thigh. Old boots, ragged stockings, torn trousers and skirts, went skating and skidding around me. The rabble closed in; I was encircled; grit flew in my face like shrapnel. Tall girls with frizzled hair, and huge boys with sharp elbows, began to prod me with hideous interest. They plucked at my scarves, spun me round like a top, screwed my nose and stole my potato.
  I was rescued at last by a gracious lady – the sixteen-year-old junior teacher – who boxed a few ears and dried my face and led me off to The Infants. I spent that first day picking holes in paper, then went home in a smouldering temper.
  'What's the matter, Lol? Didn't he like it at school then?'

'They never gave me the present.'
'Present? What present?'
'They said they'd give me a present.'
'Well, now I'm sure they didn't.'
'They did. They said : "You're Laurie Lee ain't you? Well, just you sit there for the present." I sat there all day but I never got it. I ain't going back there again!'
But after a week I felt like a veteran and grew as ruthless as anybody else. Somebody stole my baked potato, so I swiped somebody else's apple. The infant room was packed with toys such as I'd never seen before – coloured shapes and rolls of clay, stuffed birds and men to paint. Also a frame of counting beads which our young teacher played like a harp, leaning her bosom against our faces and guiding our wandering fingers ...

ACTIVITY 12

Here is another school. This one is depicted by Charles Dickens and is far less endearing! It is from *Hard Times*. What makes this school less friendly and more harsh? Can you see how the writer has manipulated your judgement by the repetition of one main idea? How effective do you think the final image is?

'Now, what I want is, Facts. Teach these boys and girls nothing but Facts. Facts alone are wanted in life. Plant nothing else, and root out everything else. You can only form minds of reasoning animals upon Facts: nothing else will ever be of any service to them. This is the principle on which I bring up these children. Stick to Facts, sir!'

The scene was a plain bare monotonous vault of a schoolroom, and the speaker's square forefinger emphasised his observations by underscoring every sentence with a line on the schoolmaster's sleeve. The emphasis was helped by the speaker's square wall of a forehead, which had his eyebrows for its base, while his eyes found commodious cellerage in two dark caves, overshadowed by the wall. The emphasis was helped by the speaker's voice which was inflexible, dry, and dictatorial. The emphasis was helped by the speaker's hair, which bristled on the skirts of his bald head, a plantation of firs to keep the wind from its shining surface, all covered with knobs, like the crust of a plum pie, as if the head had scarcely warehouse-room for the hard facts stored inside. The speaker's obstinate carriage, square coat, square legs, square shoulders – nay, his very neckcloth, trained to take him by the throat with an unaccommodating grasp, like a stubborn fact, as it was – all helped the emphasis.

'In this life, we want nothing but Facts, sir; nothing but Facts!'
The speaker, and the school master, and the third grown person present, all backed a little, and swept with their eyes the inclined plane of little vessels then and there arranged in order, ready to have imperial gallons of facts poured into them until they were full to the brim.

You might like to look at texts which describe houses, for example Bleak House in *Bleak House*, Brideshead in *Brideshead Revisited*, Pemberley in *Pride and Prejudice*. You might like to look at famous cities for example London or Oxford where stories are set. Are there any books set in your town or city or county?

So many ideas . . .

We have looked at various elements of comparison which may prove fruitful. We have glanced at comparing on the grounds of same authorship, different author but similar attitude, same time and culture, similar stock characters, similar places. All of these may prove valuable but they are probably not enough on their own. Texts must be examined from many aspects in order to provide a detailed and worthwhile comparison.

What next? How to start!

It's probably a good idea to begin with a text that you know really well and explore other texts that may be suitably linked. You could use the linked circles suggested earlier in this chapter or try the slightly different method in this activity.

ACTIVITY 13

1 Choose a text that is familiar to you and draw a spider diagram to outline and remind yourself of its main features. Here are some of the headings you could use. Write as much as you can under each heading so you can get to grips with the essence of your text.

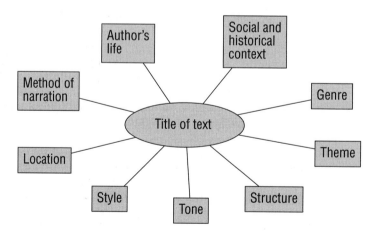

2 Now choose another text that you think may be a good one to link with your original choice. Repeat the spider diagram with the second text. Indicate which features link and which form a contrast. Keep working on this until you have really got to grips with similarities and differences. You may like to repeat the process with a third text. As you can see you will have to use many points of comparison in your essay but some will come forward as more significant than others. Refer to other chapters in this book to give you methods of comparison and strategies.

ACTIVITY 14

You could complete this phase of your research by using a checklist instead of a spider diagram.

1 Again choose a text you know well. This time compile a chart for the information. You could choose your basic text and fill in the chart and then pass the chart to another student to complete about a second text. You will, as a group, then have many different texts to consider.

Here is an example:

Aspect	Text A *Things Fall Apart*	Text B *I Know Why the Caged Bird Sings*	Significant or not?
Date published	1958	1969	
Gender of author	male	female	
Basic theme	colonisation	resilience in the face of oppression	
Genre	novel – fiction	autobiography – non-fiction	
Ethnic background	African	Black American	
Location	Nigeria	Southern United States	
Method of narration	storytelling	storytelling	
	3rd person	1st person	

2 You might like to complete the final column in the example given and discuss if the differences or similarities are significant or not. If you use this method you will be able to integrate the texts in your essay rather than treat them separately.

3 You could then look at specific incidents and analyse them. In the example above the main character in *Things Fall Apart* faces relocation and banishment from his tribe. This could be compared to Maya Angelou's reaction to her 'displacement'. Detailed study of particular passages could form the basis of the stylistic analysis. You will be given help with this in the chapter on stylistics.

Decisions, decisions

So the question was 'to link or not to link?' How, then, do you know if you have the answer? Well, the main thing to consider is, 'Does it work?'. Are there worthwhile similarities and differences which are appropriate to pursue? Do the differences or similarities help to shed light on aspects of each text? Does the comparison help to define the author's purpose or skill? Does the comparison contribute to your enjoyment and understanding of both texts?

In this chapter we have explored the nature of linked texts and thought about how we might explore these links. You will have been able to draw on what you already know. Possible bases for comparison have been highlighted and you now have some practical suggestions for getting started. More detailed methods and strategies are to be found in the rest of this book.

2 Traditions, Traditions

Genre

What does the word 'genre' mean?

Peas in a pod or files in a filing cabinet

The concept of 'genre' is rather complex. Although writers are innovative and original, obviously they are aware of previous and contemporary writers. They choose to conform to or flout conventions and tradition.

Here is a definition of genre :

A genre is an accumulation of or a tradition of practices and conventions that have come to govern the way in which particular texts are written for particular purposes.

The oldest use of the term is in literary criticism to distinguish text types: poetry, prose and drama.

(*Living Language: Language and Literature,* George Keith, Hodder & Stoughton)

In *Living Language and Literature,* George Keith and John Shuttleworth use the image of three filing cabinets labelled poetry, prose and drama. Within each filing cabinet would be a large number of files each labelled with the name of a sub-genre, for example under 'poetry' you may find *epic* and *sonnet.*

ACTIVITY 15

Divide your group into three and take a traditional genre each. Come up with as many file names for the sub-genres as you can for each of the three filing cabinets. There may be some dispute here.

For further discussion on this see *Living Language and Literature* by George Keith and John Shuttleworth (Chapter 10).

But genre isn't just about labelling texts, a relatively simple stylistics activity; it is about understanding the linguistic requirements to write effectively and read appreciatively in that genre.

Register (together with 'permitted' stylistic variation) is one of the important defining characteristics of a 'genre'.

(*Living Language and Literature,* George Keith and John Shuttleworth, Hodder & Stoughton)

COMMENTARY All literature then can be put into one of the following broad classifications: poetry, prose or drama (we'll ignore for now that you can have poetic prose and prosaic poetry!) and each one of these categories can be subdivided. Style, however, is as important as form when you are categorising genres. What makes literature vibrant or living is the variation and innovation of different writers. New genres are invented. The novel itself was a new genre in the eighteenth century. The word 'novel' comes from the Italian word *novella* meaning new, via the Latin word *novus*. Literary tradition is established when a writer chooses to 'imitate' a particular form.

Writers do not choose their genre by chance! It is a well thought out decision. A good question to ask is, 'Why did this writer choose this genre for this purpose?'

Genre can refer to subject matter, style or form. Thus the subject, *war literature* could be a genre or the *sonnet* form could be a genre.

Genre and comparison – what would you compare?

- You may find yourself comparing texts from two different genres with the same theme and show how this theme is treated differently. (The play, *Journey's End*, by R.C. Sherriff and the poems of Wilfred Owen, for example.)
- You may compare two texts from the same genre with a similar theme. (*Cider with Rosie* by Laurie Lee and *I Know Why the Caged Bird Sings* by Maya Angelou are both autobiographies or *As I Lay Dying* by William Faulkner and *Last Orders* by Graham Swift which are both concerned with funerals).
- You may be looking at two texts as examples of a genre, for example, two historical novels. (*Cold Mountain* by Charles Frazier and *Alias Grace* by Margaret Atwood).
- You may be looking at two texts to establish or disprove a genre. For example, an interesting comparison would be prequels (a work that deals with events that occur before the story told in another work) and sequels. *Wide Sargasso Sea* by Jean Rhys and *Jane Eyre* by Charlotte Brontë, *Rebecca* by Daphne du Maurier and *Mrs De Winter* by Susan Hill and also *Emma* by Jane Austen and *Emma in Love* by Emma Tennant are enjoyable examples of prequels and sequels. You may be interested in the humorous *The Book of Sequels* by Henry Beard.

ACTIVITY 16

Discuss whether you think the existence of the texts mentioned in the last point above would be enough to establish a new genre called 'prequels and sequels'? If so what are the qualities of such a genre? What would be the basis for comparison?

Dramatic genres

Tragedy, comedy, and a mixture of both called tragicomedy. These would be the files in the Drama filing cabinet. You can probably name a play by Shakespeare in each of these categories. Can you name one in each category by another playwright?

ACTIVITY 17

Shakespeare's tragedies are a sub-genre of his dramatic works. They are plays which concentrate on the downfall of one powerful character usually called the protagonist. His main tragic characters are responsible for the choices that lead to their downfall. They may have greatness but they use their strengths for evil purposes and are often justly punished for their actions.

1 Check out these features of Shakespearean tragedy to see if they hold good for a play by Shakespeare that you know well.
2 Choose another tragedy that you know well and compare its features. Is it Shakespearean or is it another sub-genre of tragedy? Some brief definitions may be useful here.

Aristotelian tragedy: Aristotle lived in the fourth century BC and he began the debate about what tragedy is. He discussed the idea of how a tragic hero in a play is neither thoroughly good nor thoroughly evil. The play itself arouses extreme emotion, which he calls pity and fear, in the audience. A mistaken action or belief is the root of the protagonist's downfall. There will be moments of revelation and reversal of fortune. Aristotle also noted that tragedy concentrated on one complete action or one event that took place in a single day and in a single place. This idea is called the three unities – the unity of time, place and action. Shakespeare follows some of these principles, but not all.

Revenge tragedy also became popular in the Elizabethan and Jacobean periods. These plays are violent and have bloodthirsty climaxes and are obviously based on vengeance. Kyd's *The Spanish Tragedy* is a good example, as is *Hamlet*.

More modern tragedies have less important people for the protagonist although they still show human failings and frailty. *Death of a Salesman* by Arthur Miller is a good example of modern tragedy.

Comedy isn't always funny

Basically the term 'comedy' when it is applied to drama means something entertaining in which no-one dies and which ends happily, often in the marriage of several characters. *Romantic comedy* involves young lovers eventually gaining their loved ones. Comedies which ridicule social behaviour can be called *satiric comedy*. A *comedy of manners* concentrates on the love intrigues of fashionable people in high society. Obviously comedy is also applied to a piece which is amusing because of the situation portrayed or because of the witty dialogue.

Tragicomedy is where potentially disastrous events are avoided and all ends happily. *The Winter's Tale* by Shakespeare is a good example. The main character, Hermione is not dead as everyone, including her husband, the King of Sicilia, thinks; she is simply hiding. The young lovers, Perdita and Florizel, eventually marry, despite all the obstacles that have been put in their way.

If you need to know more about these aspects of drama, *A Dictionary of Literary Terms* by Martin Gray (York Handbooks) is a good source of information and is clearly presented.

So you can see that drama has many different sub-genres. You could compare two tragedies showing that they are different sub-genres. You could show how Aristotle's ideas have been followed by other tragedians (or not). You could look at a tragedy and compare it to a tragicomedy. You could look at modern drama and suggest how it contrasts with earlier plays. Recurrent characters might also be a fruitful source of comparison, for example the use of country bumpkins and clever servants in both tragedy and comedy.

Whatever aspect you choose you need to have clear definitions of sub-genres and then examine particular plays in reference to these definitions.

Categories of poetry

ACTIVITY 18

Make a list of the different types of poetry you can think of which would have files in the poetry filing cabinet. You can use the information gained in the earlier activity. Begin with sonnet, lyric, narrative and see how many others you can come up with. Try to give specific examples. You could also branch out into types of versification for example free verse,

types of rhythm and rhyme quatrains, couplets and so on. You may need another drawer in your filing cabinet for these. This could be rather a long list or chart! You can see that you can compare poetry from many different angles. This is a good revision exercise as it produces a checklist and also helps you to see what you know – the feel good factor!

Comparing poems – the same but different!

ACTIVITY 19

In order to compare poetry satisfactorily you need to know something about poetic forms and poetic techniques. You will already have acquired a great deal of knowledge on this.

Here are two poems on the subject of suicide.

They have therefore a similar content but as we analyse them you will see that there are vast differences in approach. The form used is vital to the message.

Suicide in the Trenches
I knew a simple soldier boy
Who grinned at life in empty joy,
Slept soundly through the lonesome dark
And whistled early with the lark.

In winter trenches, cowed and glum,
With crumps and lice and lack of rum,
He put a bullet through his brain.
No one spoke of him again.

You smug-faced crowds with kindly eye
Who cheer when soldier lads march by,
Sneak home and pray you'll never know
The hell where youth and laughter go.

Siegfried Sassoon

This is the sad story of the suicide of a young soldier in the trenches of the First World War. It is a bitter attack on the 'smug-faced crowds' who 'sneak home'. It is a scathing and bitter commentary on people who collude in the suffering of war by cheering on the soldiers, not giving enough thought to the terrible reality of war, people who cannot imagine the 'hell where youth and laughter go'. In this poem the simple form echoes the simple innocence of the young boy. The language is simple and unassuming. There is no imagery to distract from this innocence. The simple rhyme and rhythm with their echoes of childhood cause a tension or discord between the content and the form. There is a mismatch between the simplicity and innocence of the style and the sad complexity of the content. The story is more poignant because of the simplicity of its telling.

The Suicide

And this, ladies and gentlemen, whom I am not in fact
Conducting, was his office all those minutes ago,
This man you never heard of. There are the bills
In the intray, the ash in the ashtray, the grey memoranda stacked
Against him, the serried ranks of the box files, the packed
Jury of his unanswered correspondence
Nodding under the paperweight in the breeze
From the window by which he left; and here is the cracked
Receiver that never got mended and here is the jotter
With his last doodle which might have been his own digestive tract
Ulcer and all or might be the flowery maze
Through which he had wandered deliciously till he stumbled
Suddenly finally conscious of all he lacked
On a manhole under the hollyhocks. The pencil
Point had obviously broken, yet, when he left this room
By catdrop sleight-of-foot or simple vanishing act,
To those who knew him for all that mess in the street
This man with the shy smile has left behind
Something that was intact.

Louis MacNeice

This poem recounts the death of a friend or an acquaintance of the poet. It is the story of the complexity and stress of everyday life for some people and shows their inability to cope. Their cries for help are unheeded.

1 List the similarities in content and theme of these poems. Then list the differences in content and theme.
2 Now look carefully at the style and form. This is where you can see how very different the treatment of the theme is. Look at rhyme, line ends, imagery, formality of language. (Give precise examples to prove your point). Comment on how easy the poems are to understand. You will need to look at the structure of the poems, where the lines end, how long the sentences are, if there are any double meanings or obscure references.

The poets treat their subject matter very differently here and the actual form of the poem is part of the intricate message of each poem.

Revelations

Dramatic monologues are intriguing texts to examine. They can be found in poetry, prose and drama. This demonstrates how complex categorising can be. A dramatic monologue is a text where the person speaking in the text (not the writer) is addressing the listener/reader and the listener/reader learns more about the speaker than the speaker acknowledges about himself.

Good examples of dramatic monologues include the series of short plays *Talking Heads* by Alan Bennett and the poems 'In Westminster Abbey' by John Betjeman, 'The Hawk Roosting' by Ted Hughes and the two studies of murderers 'My Last Duchess' and 'Porphyria's Lover' by Robert Browning.

ACTIVITY 20

Find copies of two of these texts and show how the writer has created the characters.

You should be able to make a detailed character sketch of the speakers.

Categories of prose

This is a complex category. There are many different types of prose. The first distinction to be made is between fiction and non-fiction.

Even this is now a statement that is debatable! An article by George Keith in *e-magazine* (Issue 9 September 2000) suggests that the distinction between and fiction and non-fiction should be examined carefully. In his lively and thought-provoking article Keith suggests that the distinction implies that non-fiction is a 'second class' form of writing – it suggests a sort of apartheid where fiction is supreme and the rest is lumped together and not worth anything much simply because it is *not* fiction. In his article Keith puts forward four alternative classifications for modes of writing/genres/text types.

1 Narrative – history, biography, travel, short stories, poetry and sciences.
2 Reflection – discursive writing, commentary (not the sporting kind).
3 Dialogue – novels, plays, biography, newspapers.
4 Argument – a point of view presented for consideration: poetry, political manifestos, articles.

This new classification cuts across 'the great divide' of fiction and non-fiction.

ACTIVITY 21

Here are outlines of several texts. In groups, discuss them and try to fit each of the texts into this new classification system.

(a) *The Floating Brothel.* A book about the conditions on board the first shiploads of convicts to reach Australia in 1790.

(b) *Going, Going.* A poem by Philip Larkin which shows how we are polluting our planet.
(c) Alan Bennett's monologues, *Talking Heads.*
(d) *The Prelude.* Wordsworth's long autobiographical poem about his spiritual and physical growth.

(e) *Paradise Lost* by John Milton. An account of Satan and the Fall of Man written as an epic poem 'to justify the ways of God to Man'.

(f) A magazine article about the benefits of exercise.

(g) A selection of poetry about the effects of war.

(h) A novel portraying how badly the indigenous people of a new colony were treated.

(i) A travel book which points out the good and bad things about a country.

Can you think of any more categories and examples? This is not as clear cut as it looks but then the traditional categories are not that easy either!

ACTIVITY 22

1 Here is the beginning of a chart. Fill in some of the blanks showing the different categories of prose texts in the traditional classification of 'fiction' and 'non-fiction' that you can think of. You may need to think first about specific texts you have studied and try to categorise those. Can you supply an example of each one?

Fiction (The novel)	Non-fiction
Historical	Biographical
Romance	Encyclopaedia
Science Fiction	Instruction Manual
Gothic	
Epistolary	

2 When you have done this notice how discerning you have been. Is Science Fiction about aliens landing on earth in the present time in the same genre as science fiction based in the future? Is a spoof Gothic novel like *Northanger Abbey* by Jane Austen the same genre as *The Mysteries of Udolpho* by Ann Radcliffe and Mary Shelley's *Frankenstein*? Is a historical novel about famous characters in the same genre as one about unknown people in the past?

Stranger than fiction

There is also another genre which you may have come across. This is called *faction* or *reportage*. This straddles fiction and non-fiction. George Keith would call it *narrative*.

ACTIVITY 23

Examples of reportage are *In Cold Blood* by Truman Capote, *Schindler's Ark* and *The Playmaker,* both by Thomas Keneally.

1 Find summaries of the stories of these texts from the blurb on the covers or on the Internet.

2 Brainstorm what sources a writer might find useful, for example, newspaper stories or diaries.

3 Obtain copies of these texts if you can and note down what actual sources have been used.

A good comparison could be made by looking at how these sources have been used by the writer and the effect this has on the text and also on the reader.

Changing places

Notice also that these categories can cross over, with an autobiography being written in poetic form (Wordsworth's *Prelude*) or in prose (*I Know Why the Caged Bird Sings* by Maya Angelou and *Cider with Rosie* by Laurie Lee). There are also fictional autobiographies like *Great Expectations* and *Jane Eyre* as well as 'true stories'. So within each branch of prose there is a great variety of sub-genres.

So, then, a genre can be defined by subject matter or form. It can also be defined in terms of tone, for example comic, tragic, satirical. The difficulty in classification keeps literature alive through inspirations with new innovations always being developed.

A closer look

In your work in Activity 22, you may have come up with *Bildungsroman* as a genre – there again you may not! This is a German word which can be literally translated as 'formation novel' – it describes a text in which the main character 'grows up'. You may have come up with autobiography both fictional and non-fictional. You may have come up with travel writing …

It is these three categories of writing that we can look at in detail here. By looking at how to compare these types of texts, you will develop analytical skills which can be transferred to other types of texts.

So what does Bildungsroman mean?

Let us look first at *Bildungsroman*. You were probably curious enough to have looked this up but just in case … a *Bildungsroman* is a novel which follows the fortunes and misfortunes of the main character from childhood to maturity. It can be a fictional autobiography or a simple third person narrative.

Emma by Jane Austen and *Jane Eyre* by Charlotte Brontë are good examples of novels which show the development of the main character. *Jane Eyre* is written in the first person and *Emma* in the third person although both give a clear insight into the thoughts and feelings of the main characters. Obviously we cannot examine the whole of these in any great detail. If you have read both novels you may be able to list the similarities and differences and see if you could link and compare the texts on the basis of genre alone. It is probable that you could do some useful comparison but you will soon realise that texts need to be compared from several different angles to make a fully satisfying comparison.

In both of these novels the main character undergoes a traumatic experience after a shocking revelation. You may know that Jane Eyre discovers that the man she is in church with and is about to marry has a mad wife at home and that Emma discovers that she has been in love with a family friend without realising it until it looks as if someone else wants to marry him! The revelations are agonising for the main characters.

ACTIVITY 24

1 Here are extracts from these novels which describe the feelings of the main characters. Look carefully at them and note their similarities. You might like to concentrate on how the thoughts and feelings are indicated.
2 What is the structure of the extracts?
3 Now look at the differences in language use.

Which one seems more formal? What do you learn of the characters of the two women in these extracts? Jane is desolate while Emma is more humiliated. Prove this statement.
4 How is Jane's desolation expressed? How is Emma's humiliation expressed?

Jane Eyre
Jane is in her room. It is her wedding day. In the church earlier the ceremony was interrupted by a man claiming that Rochester, her husband to be, was already married. It is stated that his present wife is locked up in the house. Her narrative is in the first person.

I was in my own room as usual – just myself, without obvious change: nothing had smitten me or scathed me, or maimed me. And yet where was the Jane Eyre of yesterday? – where was her life? where were her prospects?

Jane Eyre, who had been an ardent, expectant woman – almost a bride – was a cold solitary girl again: her life was pale, her prospects were desolate. A Christmas frost had come at midsummer; a white December storm had whirled over June; ice glazed the ripe apples, drifts crushed the blowing roses; on hay field and cornfield lay a frozen shroud: lanes which last night blushed full of flowers, today were pathless with untrodden snow; and the woods which twelve hours since waved leafy and fragrant as groves between the tropics, now spread, waste, wild and white as pine-forests in wintry Norway. My hopes were all dead-struck with a subtle doom, such as in one night, fell on all the first born in the land of Egypt ...

Some time in the afternoon I raised my head, and looking round and seeing the western sun gilding the sign of its decline upon the wall I asked, 'what am I to do?'

But the answer my mind gave – 'leave Thornfield at once' – was so prompt, so dread, that I stopped my ears: I said, I could not bear such words now. 'That I am not Edward Rochester's bride is the least part of my woe.' I alleged: that I have awakened out of most glorious dreams, and found them all void and vain, is a horror I could bear and master; but that I must leave him decidedly, instantly, entirely is intolerable. I cannot do it.

Emma
The extract from *Emma* is in the third person but restricted to the viewpoint of Emma. In fact the whole novel is in this vein. This enables the reader to interpret the thoughts and feelings of the main character including her self-delusion. Emma has realised for the first time what the reader has been guessing – that she is in love with Mr Knightley.

The rest of the day, the following night, were hardly enough for her thoughts. She was bewildered amidst the confusion of all that had rushed on her within the last few hours. Every moment had brought a fresh surprise: and every surprise must be a matter of humiliation for her. How to understand it all! How to understand the deceptions she had been thus practising on herself and living under! The blunders, the blindness of her own head and heart. She sat still, she walked about, she tried her own room, she tried the shrubbery – in every place, every posture, she perceived that she had acted most weakly; that she had been imposed on by others in a most mortifying degree; that she had been imposing on herself in a degree yet more mortifying; that she was wretched and should probably find this day but the beginning of wretchedness ...

How long had Mr Knightley been so dear to her, as every feeling declared him now to be? When had his influence, such influence begun?

COMMENTARY

Notice that Jane seems to be two people in this extract. She refers to herself as the 'Jane Eyre of yesterday' and talks of 'she' rather than 'I'. This demonstrates her disbelief and anxiety. The events of the day have made her a different person.

Emma repeats the ideas of confusion, bewilderment and surprise. She repeats the words 'mortifying' and 'wretched' as if she cannot believe what has happened. She is full of self doubt and questions her behaviour. Here the third person narrative is used because that is the point of view from which the book is written but here it also gives the impression of the character stepping outside herself to judge her actions.

ACTIVITY 25

1 Which one represents more vividly the feelings of the character in your opinion? Convert the extract from *Emma* into the first person and decide if this would have been a more effective way of telling the story.
2 Consider the advantages of a first and third person narrative. Which one gives a clearer understanding of character in your opinion? Which method engages the reader more and why? The effect of viewpoint on a text would be a good starting point for linking or contrasting texts.

Autobiography – fiction or fact?

It could be said that all autobiography is partly fiction. How many times have we told a story about our experiences and embroidered the truth somewhat? If we heard a friend retelling an event would we use the same language and put the same slant on it? Time changes our perceptions. How often have you been distressed by an event and then later retold it in an amusing way? Autobiography is often like this with the writer looking on the bright side or deliberately changing the perspective of an event. There are also fictional 'autobiographies' in which the narrator is a fictional character. Frequently the real events in the author's life feature prominently through the activities and experiences of fictional characters. There are many events in *David Copperfield* which Dickens experienced first hand. It is, in some of its details, Dickens' veiled autobiography. It is fairly obvious that writers write about situations they have experienced!

The truth, the whole truth and nothing but the truth!

Let us first consider *real* autobiographies.

Three autobiographies will be considered here. You may be familiar with some of them. *Oleander, Jacaranda* by Penelope Lively is about her childhood in Egypt and gives a clear picture of British colonial life in the 1930s and 1940s. *I Know Why the Caged Bird Sings* by Maya Angelou tells of her early life in the Southern States of America in the 1930s. *Cider with Rosie* is about the early life of Laurie Lee in a remote Cotswold village in the 1920s. The two latter writers published their autobiographies in several volumes and we will only be considering the first in the series.

ACTIVITY 26

Discuss these questions before you begin to study specific autobiographies.

1 What would you expect any child to encounter in the first dozen years of life? Make a list of likely events. This is then the fundamental basis of these texts.
2 What different experiences would you expect to happen in Gloucestershire, the Southern States of the USA and Egypt?
3 One black and two white, two females and one male. What factors would influence experiences? When you have established what you might expect you can then check the text to see if this is covered in the content.

Further thoughts on autobiography

Of necessity there will much reflection and some discussion in the text. The style may vary between the sophisticated language of an established writer and the childlike language associated with the events of childhood. How would you begin to link and compare these texts? Try to come up with a checklist of avenues to explore.

Your list might have looked something like this.

■ A list of the main events that are typical of childhood which occur in all the texts.
■ A list of specific events which are restricted to one text because of its setting or time.
■ A detailed look at the beginning or end of the texts.
■ A detailed look at the varieties of language used. Is it formal, informal, childlike or adult? Plain or figurative?
■ A comparison of the tones. Are they reflective, humorous, bitter, sentimental or a mixture of many attitudes?
■ Are there any events which seem exaggerated or unreal?
■ An examination of the character of the subject of the autobiography i.e. the narrator/author.
■ Discussion of significant people and events in the life of the subject of the autobiography.
■ The order of the events. Does it need to be strictly chronological? Is it likely that it would be? Discuss possible structures.
■ A detailed look at the style of a specific turning point in the story.
■ A consideration of what impression the reader builds up of the social and political background to the subject's life.

First memories

Think about your earliest memories. What are they? Was it your first day at school? The birth of a brother or sister? Moving house? Being hurt? Being lost? This would be the beginning of your autobiography!

The beginning of any piece of literature is vitally important to its success. Readers do not continue unless they are interested or their curiosity is aroused. Here are the beginnings of the three autobiographies under discussion.

The first is an extract from the prologue to *I Know Why the Caged Bird Sings*. Maya as child in church has been called upon to recite a poem. In the prologue to her autobiography she shows how she felt she was a white beauty locked up in the ugly body of a black girl – by the end of the book she has become proud to be black but as a child she resented her background and colour. The second part of the extract is the beginning of Chapter One.

Extract One

Wouldn't they be surprised when one day I woke out of my black ugly dream, and my real hair, which was long and blond, would take the place of the kinky mass that Momma wouldn't let me straighten? My light blue eyes were going to hypnotize them, after all the things they said about 'my daddy must have been a Chinaman' (I thought they meant made out of china, like a cup) because my eyes were small and squinty. Then they would understand why I had never picked up a Southern accent, or spoke the common slang, and why I had to be forced to eat pigs' tails and snouts. Because I was really white and because a cruel fairy stepmother, who was understandably jealous of my beauty, had turned me into a too-big Negro girl with nappy black hair, broad feet and a space between her teeth that would hold a number-two pencil . . .

. . . 'What you looking . . .' The minister's wife leaned towards me, her long yellow face full of sorry. She whispered, 'I just come to tell you, it's Easter Day.' I repeated, jamming the words together, 'Ijustcometotellyouit'sEaster-day', as low as possible. The giggles hung in the air like melting clouds that were waiting to rain on me. I held up two fingers, close to my chest, which meant that I had to go to the toilet, and tiptoed toward the rear of the church. Dimly, somewhere over my head, I heard ladies saying 'Lord bless the child,' and 'Praise God'. My head was up and my eyes were open, but I didn't see anything. Halfway down the aisle, the church exploded with 'Were you there when they crucified my Lord?' and I tripped over a foot stuck out from the children's pew. I stumbled and started to say something, or maybe scream, but a green persimmon, or it could have been a lemon, caught me between the legs and squeezed. I tasted sour on my tongue and felt it at the back of my mouth. Then before I reached the door, the sting was burning down my legs and into my Sunday socks. I tried to hold, to squeeze it back, to keep it from speeding, but when I reached the church porch I knew I'd have to let it go, or it would probably run right back up to my head and my poor head would burst like a dropped watermelon, and all the brains and spit and tongue and eyes would roll all over the place. So I ran down into the yard and let it go. I ran, peeing and crying, not toward the toilet out back but to our house. I'd get a whipping for it to be sure, and the nasty children would have something new to tease me about. I laughed anyway, partially for the sweet release; still, the greater joy came not only from being liberated from the silly church but from the knowledge that I wouldn't die from a busted head.

If growing up is painful for the Southern Black girl, being aware of the displacement is the rust on the razor that threatens the throat. It is an unnecessary insult.

Chapter One

When I was three and Bailey four, we had arrived in the musty little town, wearing tags on our wrists which instructed – 'To Whom It May Concern' – that we were Marguerite and Bailey Johnson Jr, from Long Beach, California, en route to Stamps, Arkansas, c/o Mrs Annie Henderson.

Our parents had decided to put an end to their calamitous marriage, and father shipped us home to his mother. A porter had been charged with our welfare – he got off the train the next day in Arizona – and our tickets were pinned to my brother's inside coat pocket.

I don't remember much of the trip, but after we reached the segregated southern part of the journey, things must have looked up. Negro passengers, who always travelled with loaded lunch boxes, felt sorry for 'the poor little motherless darlings' and plied us with cold fried chicken and potato salad.

Years later I discovered that the United States had been crossed thousands of times by frightened black children travelling alone to their newly affluent parents in Northern cities, or back to grandmothers in Southern towns when the urban North reneged on its economic promises.

The town reacted to us as its inhabitants had reacted to all things new before our coming. It regarded us a while without curiosity but with caution, and after we were seen to be harmless (and children) it closed in around us, as a real mother embraces a stranger's child. Warmly but not too familiarly.

We lived with our grandmother and uncle in the rear of the Store (it was always spoken of with a capital s), which she had owned for some twenty-five years.

Early in the century, Momma (we soon stopped calling her Grandmother) sold lunches to the sawmen in the lumberyard (East Stamps) and the seedmen at the cotton gin (West Stamps). Her crisp meat pies and cool lemonade, when joined to her miraculous ability to be in two places at the same time, assured her of business success. From being a mobile lunch counter, she had set up a stand between the two points of fiscal interest and supplied the workers' needs for a few years. Then she had the store built in the heart of the Negro area. Over the years it became the lay centre of activities in the town. On Saturdays, barbers sat their customers in the shade on the porch of the store, and troubadours on their ceaseless crawlings through the South leaned across its benches and sang their sad songs of the Brazos while they played their juice harps and cigar-box guitars.

COMMENTARY In this opening we get an extremely clear idea of her thoughts as a child but also some insight into her thoughts as an adult with the mature reflection that adulthood brings. She thought she was too good to be black. Her 'black' existence seemed like a dream to her and her real hair was long and blond and her eyes were blue. She never spoke the 'common slang' and didn't enjoy the delicacies of her contemporaries which were pigs' snouts and tails. She was teased by the other children because of her attitude which is not surprising.

She demonstrates her childish fantasies by mentioning that her 'cruel fairy stepmother' had turned her from her beautiful white self into a 'too-big Negro girl with nappy black hair and a space between her teeth that would hold a number two pencil'. No doubt this is a fairly accurate description of her appearance as a child. Notice the marked order of 'black' in 'my black ugly dream'. Her other childish fantasies are shown in her belief that her 'wee' would 'run right back up to (her) head' which would 'burst like a dropped watermelon and all the brains and spit and tongue and eyes would roll all over the place.' The watermelon simile is effective and well within her experience as a child. The detail of the anatomical results is also childish and vivid. A more sophisticated simile describes the children's giggles as 'like melting clouds that were waiting to rain on me', a curious assimilation of sound, sight and touch. One of the most vivid metaphors in the book is the one describing her feeling of displacement as 'the rust on the razor that threatens the throat'.

The childhood experiences are described here in a very sensuous way. The stinging 'wee' was 'burning' down her legs and 'tasted sour'. Her Momma made 'crisp meat pies' and 'cool lemonade'.

The passage shows a sense of humour which also comes with maturity. Her father was thought by the children to be a Chinaman because of her 'squinty eyes'. Maya 'thought they meant made out of china like a cup.' We have to smile at the simple statement 'a porter had been charged with our welfare – he got off the train the next day'. Also her rendering of the poem with all the words jammed together brings a smile to the reader's face. Apart from the humour we also notice the hard life she had as she realises she will get a whipping for her behaviour in church and the way she acknowledges the teasing by the other children.

There is also the obvious mixture of childlike and adult language in phrases such as 'silly church' and 'nasty' children but also 'calamitous marriage', 'newly affluent parents', and what happened when the 'urban North reneged on its economic promises.' The extract is written in the first person and the past tense.

In this brief commentary the thoughts, imagery, appeals to the senses, tone and language have been touched on.

Extract Two

Oleander, Jacaranda by Penelope Lively

We are going by car from Bulaq Dakhur to Heliopoplis. I am in the back. The leather of the seats sticks to my bare legs. We travel along a road lined at either side with oleader and jacaranda trees, alternate splashes of white and blue. I chant quietly: 'Jacaranda, oleander . . . Jacaranda, oleander . . .' And as I do so there comes to me the revelation that in a few hour's time we shall return by the same route and that I shall pass the same trees in reverse order – oleander, jacaranda, oleander, jacaranda – and that by the same token, I can look back upon myself of now, of this moment now thinking this – but it will be then not now.

   And in due course I did so, and perceived with excitement the chasm between past and future, the perpetual slide of the present. As, writing this, I think with equal wonder of that irretrievable child, and of the eerie relationship between her mind and mine. She is myself, but a self which is unreachable except by means of such miraculously surviving moments of being: the alien within. Here is a child thinking about time, experiencing a sudden illumination about chronology and a person's capacity for reflection. In terms of developmental psychology, this would seem to be significant, an indication of a particular achievement – the ability to be actively concerned with the general nature of things. But the findings and discussion of developmental psychology can make oddly frustrating reading – they reflect the process of scientific observation and are hence illuminating, but they seem to have no apparent bearing on the rainbow experience we have all lost, but of which we occasionally retrieve a brilliant glimpse. I know now what was going on in my head that lay over fifty years ago. I can turn the cold eye of adult knowledge and experience upon the moment and interpret it in the light of a lifetime's reading and reflection. But what seems most astonishing of all is that something of the reality of the moment survives this destructive freight of wisdom and rationality, firmly hitched to the physical world. In my mind there is still the tacky sensation of the leather car seat which sticks to the back of my knees. I see still the bright flower laden trees. I roll the lavish names around on the tongue: 'Jacaranda, oleander . . .' for this is an incident infused with the sense of language quite as much as with the perception of the nature of time: the possession and control of these decorative words, the satisfaction of being able to say them, display them. Though all this was done, I know in privacy: this interesting perception, the significance of it and the excitement, had to be mine alone, uncommunicated. And now, appropriately, the adult with whom I share it is myself.

Extract Three

Cider with Rosie by Laurie Lee

I was set down from the carrier's cart at the age of three; and with a sense of bewilderment and terror my life in the village began. The June grass, amongst which I stood, was taller than I was, and I wept. I had never been so close to grass before. It towered above me and all around me, each blade tattooed with tiger skins of sunlight. It was knife edged, dark, and wicked green, thick as a forest and alive with grasshoppers that chirped and chattered and leapt through the air like monkeys.

I was lost and didn't know where to move. A tropic heat oozed up from the ground, rank with sharp odours of roots and nettles. Snow-clouds of elder blossom banked in the sky, showering upon me the fumes and flakes of their sweet and giddy suffocation. High overhead ran frenzied larks, screaming, as though the sky were tearing apart.

For the first time in my life I was out of sight of humans. For the first time in my life I was alone in a world whose behaviour I could neither predict nor fathom; a world of birds that squealed, of plants that stank, of insects that sprang about without warning. I was lost and I did not expect to be found again. I put back my head and howled, and the sun hit me smartly in the face like a bully.

From this daylight nightmare I was awakened, as from many another, by the appearance of my sisters. They came scrambling and calling up the steep rough bank, and parting the long grass found me. Faces of rose, familiar, living; huge shining faces hung up like shields between me and the sky; faces with grins and white teeth (some broken) to be conjured up like genii with a howl, brushing off terror with their scoldings and affection. They leaned over me – one, two, three – their mouths smeared with red currants and their hands dripping with juice. 'There, there it's all right, don't you wail anymore. Come down 'ome and we'll stuff you with currants' and Marjorie the eldest, lifted me into her long brown hair, and ran me jogging down the path and through the steep rose-filled garden, and set me down on the cottage doorstep, which was our home, though I couldn't believe it.

That was the day we came to our village, in the summer of the last year of the First World War. To a cottage that stood in a half acre of garden on a steep bank above a lake; a cottage with three floors and a cellar and a treasure in the walls, with a pump and apple trees, syringa and strawberries, rooks in the chimneys, frogs in the cellar, mushrooms on the ceiling, and all for three and sixpence a week.

ACTIVITY 27

1 Read the extracts carefully. All three show that the children are displaced in some way. You might find the following guidelines helpful when you study them in detail.
   i) Compare the use of the senses in these three openings. Look for appeals to sight, touch, sound, taste and smell.
   ii) Compare the use of language. Find examples of dialect. Look at the use of figurative language.
   iii) Which one gives the most effective account of a child's earliest memories? Which one is the most reflective?
   iv) Compare what you learn about the social and political background of each of these autobiographies.

Getting organised

2 Make a chart like the one below which will enable you to do a detailed comparison of these texts. Tick the aspects which are found and provide evidence. Some examples have been entered already. You may find other aspects of the texts to compare.

Aspect of text	*Cider with Rosie*	*I Know Why the Caged Bird Sings*	*Oleander, Jacaranda*
Childlike language		'all the brains and spit and tongue and eyes would roll all over the place'	
Appeals to the senses; sight sound touch taste smell			'The leather of the seat sticks to my bare legs'
Reflective language			
Adult language			
Figurative language	'like a bully' 'faces like shields'	'giggles like melting clouds'	
Humour		'I thought they meant made out of china like a cup'	
General social comment or background information.		'I'd get a whipping for it to be sure'	
Characters other than the narrator			

Which autobiography would you most want to continue reading?

Definitely not the truth

Some novels are written as if they are autobiographies. These can be called fictional autobiographies. They could be compared by the same method.

ACTIVITY 28

Here are the beginnings of two fictional autobiographies. Use the chart above to begin to examine these extracts. Adapt the 'aspect of text' column if you think something else would be more appropriate.

Moll Flanders by Daniel Defoe

My true name is so well known in the records or registers at Newgate, and in the Old Bailey, and there are some things of such consequence still depending there, relating to my particular conduct, that it is not to be expected that I should set my name or the account of my family to this work; perhaps after my death it may be better known; at present it would not be proper, no, not though a general pardon should be issued, even without exceptions of persons or crimes.

It is enough to tell you, that as some of my worst comrades who are out of the way of doing me harm (having gone out of the world by the steps and the string, as I often expected them to go), knew me by the name of Moll Flanders, so you may give me leave to go under that name till I dare own who I have been, as well as who I am.

I have been told, that in one of our neighbour nations, whether it be in France or elsewhere I know not, they have an order from the king, that when any criminal is condemned, either to die, or to the galleys, or to be transported, if they leave any children, as such are generally unprovided for, by the forfeiture of their parents, so they are immediately taken into the care of the government, and put into a hospital called the house of orphans, where they are bred up, clothed, fed, taught, and when fit to go out, are placed to trades, or to services, so as to be well able to provide for themselves by an honest, industrious behaviour.

Had this been the custom in our country, I had not been left a poor desolate girl without friends, without clothes, without help or helper, as was my fate; and by which I was not only exposed to very great distresses, even before I was capable either of understanding my case or how to amend it, but brought into a course of life, scandalous in itself, and which in its ordinary course tended to the swift destruction both of soul and body.

But the case was otherwise here. My mother was convicted of felony for petty theft, scarce worth naming, viz. borrowing three pieces of fine holland of a certain draper in Cheapside. The circumstances are too long to repeat, and I have heard them related in many ways, that I can scarce tell which is the right account.

However they all agree in this, that my mother pleaded her belly, and being found quick with child, she was respited for about seven months; after which she was called down, as they term it, to her former judgement, but obtained the favour afterwards of being transported to the plantations, and left me about half a year old, and in bad hands you may be sure.

This is too near the first hours of my life for me to relate anything of myself but hearsay; 'tis enough to mention, that as I was born in such an unhappy place, I had no parish to have recourse to for my nourishment in my infancy; nor can I give the least account of how I was kept alive, other than that, as I have been told, some relation of my mother took me away, but at whose expense and at whose direction, I know nothing at all of it.

Here is the beginning of *David Copperfield* by
Charles Dickens:

> Whether I shall turn out to be the hero of my own life, or whether that station will be held by anyone else, these pages must show. To begin my life with the beginning of my life, I record that I was born (as I have been informed and believe) on Friday, at twelve o'clock at night. It was remarked that the clock began to strike as I began to cry simultaneously.
>
> In consideration of the day and hour of my birth, it was declared by the nurse, and by some sage women in the neighbourhood who had taken a lively interest in me several months before there was possibility of our becoming personally acquainted, first that I was destined to be unlucky in life; and secondly, that I was privileged to see ghosts and spirits; both these gifts inevitably attaching, as they believed to all unlucky infants of either gender, born towards the small hours on a Friday night.
>
> I need say nothing here on the first head, because nothing can show better than my history whether that prediction was verified or falsified by the result. On the second branch of the question, I will only remark that unless I ran through that part of my inheritance while I was still a baby, I have not come into it yet. But I do not at all complain of having been kept out of property; and if anyone else should be in present enjoyment of it, he is heartily welcome to keep it.

You could look at *The Catcher in the Rye* by
J.D. Salinger if you would like another fictional
autobiography to work on.

The new travel guides

A genre that is becoming more popular is travel writing. This is because travel is now easier and cheaper than ever before. In fact Bill Bryson's book *Notes From a Small Island* was a bestseller for years only to be replaced by his book about Australia, *Down Under*. An increase in world travel and adventure holidays has made travel guides big business. To some extent it was a stroke of genius by Bill Bryson to write about that under-explored island of Great Britain mostly for a British audience. Lonely Planet and Rough Guides tell the reader where to go and what to do. Literary travel writing gives the reader a personal impression and opinion of places and people. Here we shall confine ourselves to a study of travel writing about Britain.

An early travel book is *A Tour through the Whole Island of Great Britain* by Daniel Defoe. This was originally published in 1742. This is now considered a social document but in its time it was a popular guide book. Here is an extract from the introduction to the Everyman's Library edition, published by Dent in 1962:

> He put into it not merely the usual description of historic places and buildings, seats of noblemen and gentlemen who were the unquestioned political rulers of the England of his day, picturesque scenes and anecdotes after the fashion of the times, and travellers' information of the approved sort, but also things that interested him, and seemed to him significant of the great social transition he saw proceeding around him. So much did these latter things concern him that he was often perfunctory, and not seldom inaccurate, in providing the customary tourist's fare ...

Defoe himself, in his preface, wrote:

If this work is not both pleasant and profitable to the reader, the author most freely and openly declares the fault must be in his performance, and it cannot be any deficiency in the subject.

As the work itself is a description of the most flourishing and opulent country in the world, so there is a flowing variety of materials; all the particulars are fruitful of instructing and diverting objects.

If novelty pleases, here is the present state of the country described, the improvement, as well in culture, as in commerce, the encrease of people, and employment for them: also here you have an account of the encrease of buildings, as well in great cities and towns, as in the new seats and dwellings of the nobility and gentry; also the encrease of wealth, in many eminent particulars.

If antiquity takes with you, tho' looking back into remote things is studiously avoided, yet it is not wholly omitted, nor any useful observations neglected.

It would be interesting to see if the modern travel writers have the same qualities. It would also be interesting to speculate if *Notes from a Small Island* will still be available in print nearly 250 years after its publication!

Is it better to travel hopefully than to arrive?

The books we shall be considering are *Notes From A Small Island* by Bill Bryson, *The Kingdom by the Sea* by Paul Theroux, *Broke through Britain* by Peter Mortimer and *Home Truths* by Bill Murphy.

ACTIVITY 29

Here are the blurbs for three of these books. The blurb is the writing on the back cover of the book that you read before you decide if you want to buy it or not. As a group activity study these blurbs and make a list of the purpose of each travel book. Suggest what effect a different purpose might have on the style, content and structure of the book. Suggest the tone of each text from the hints given in the blurb. (You can describe tone with words like *satirical, humorous, critical, admiring, bitter, delighted*.) Think carefully about Mortimer's book and the effect of the conditions in which he undertakes the journey. You may come to the conclusion that his journey is as much spiritual as it is physical.

Notes From A Small Island

After nearly two decades in Britain, Bill Bryson took the decision to move back to the States for a while, to let his kids experience life in another country, to give his wife a chance to shop until 10pm seven nights a week, and, most of all, because he had read that 3.7 million Americans believed that they had been abducted by aliens at one time or another, and it was thus clear to him that his people needed him.

But before leaving his much-loved home in North Yorkshire, Bryson insisted on taking one last trip round Britain, a sort of valedictory tour of the green and kindly island that had so long been his home. His aim was to take stock of the nation's public face and private parts (as it were), and to analyse what precisely it was he loved so much about a country that had produced Marmite, a military hero whose dying wish was to be kissed by a fellow named Hardy, place names like Farleigh Wallop, Titsey and Shellow Bowells, people who said 'Mustn't grumble', and *Gardeners' Question Time*.

The Kingdom by the Sea

From the white cliffs of Dover to Cornwall and Wales, on to Ulster and Scotland, Paul Theroux sets out on a three month journey around Britain's coast. In the bestselling tradition of *The Old Patagonian Express*, he presents a vivid portrait of a complex country and its people ... decent, quirky, private, baffling, and endlessly eccentric.

Broke through Britain

During the summer of 1998, Peter Mortimer set off on the 500 mile journey from Plymouth to Edinburgh, accompanied only by his King Charles spaniel. He took no money and had no transport or pre-arranged accommodation. Bereft of the basics necessary for human existence, such as food and shelter, he was dependent for survival on his own wits, the generosity of others and good fortune.

Broke through Britain is a record of both the physical and mental demands such an undertaking placed on Mortimer, and it offers a humorous, poignant and oblique slant on our national characteristics at the dawn of the new millennium. Peter Mortimer gives a vivid account of life lived on the fringes of society in a country where there is an ever-increasing gulf between the rich and the poor. It is a genuine adventure into the unknown – not in some remote, hostile land, but here on our own doorstep. He may even have landed on yours.

ACTIVITY 30

1 Here are the endings of three of the texts. From the blurbs given above can you identify which is which? The answers are at the end of this chapter.
2 Look in more detail at the style of the texts. What can you say about the language and tone of them? You should look at aspects such as sentence length and type (questions or statements), repetition and patterning. Try to think of some words to describe the tone which have not yet been mentioned in this chapter!

Text A

The journey was not easy. Nor was writing the book. Early drafts seemed over-gloomy, dwelling on the depressive aspects. Who'd want to read such self-pitying whines? I tried to inject some humour. Was it too much? Did it dilute the experience? And was I merely skating across a 500-mile surface? I had no research, no statistics, no foreknowledge. I was merely one flawed human being trudging across a changing terrain and responding with a notebook.

My mental state was often strange, my mind and body fatigued. Witness how many factual errors in the manuscript were unearthed by my excellent editor at Mainstream, Cathy Mineards. And me an ex-journalist ...

In all of us there is a restlessness, a sense that there should be more to life, that it should be different from how it is. This restlessness will not go away. Nor will it ever be satisfied. All we have is the trying. And after that the trying again.

Text B

What an enigma will Britain seem to historians when they look back on the second half of the twentieth century. Here is a country that fought and won a noble war, dismantled a mighty empire in a generally benign and enlightened way, creating a far-seeing welfare state – in short, did nearly everything right. The fact is that this is still the best place in the world for most things – to post a letter, go for a walk, watch television, buy a book, venture out for a drink, go to a museum, use the bank, get lost, seek help, or stand on a hillside and take in a view.

All of this came to me in the space of a lingering moment. I've said it before and I'll say it again. I like it here. I like it more than I can tell you. And then I turned from the gate and got into the car and knew without doubt that I would be back.

Text C

Today I was done – I had no plans. Over there, across the Thames estuary at Margate, I had set out almost three months ago. It was not far across the river mouth – less than thirty miles. So I had made a connection. I had found a way of joining one end of this kingdom to the other, giving it a beginning and an end. I would not have done it differently in Africa. I felt I knew the world much better for having seen Britain – and I knew Britain so well and had been in its pockets so long, I felt impatient to leave; I had my usual bad dream that I would be forced to stay longer.

The tide came in. I was still at the end of the pier. I had never seen a tide rise so fast, from so far away.

I could see it flowing across the foreshore as if it were being poured. It became a rippling flood. Now after a few minutes it was a foot deep. It was moving the boats, buoying them, rocking them on their keels. I saw a shallow dinghy, just like the one I had rowed from Bellanaleck to Carrybridge, across Lough Erne, past people standing in wet fields who were living their lives there. I had rowed back and forth, and then had gone away. Every day on the coast I had gone away, leaving people staring out at the ocean's crowded chop: 'Our end is Life – put out to sea'.

The rising tide took the smell away. Then the gulls flew off – and that was another thing about travel: these flights, these disappearances. It was no different in Britain from any other foreign place, except that a country could sound sad if you spoke the language.

Fish were jumping where there had been coils of rope sinking in the mud and the bubble holes. The boats were straightening and creaking. Now the sea was splashing against the pier. I sat there until all the boats were upright, even those big peeling motor launches. One hulk had been holed and did not rise – the water lapped at the roof of its wheel house. I did not want to think of a name for it. The tide was high. I started down the long pier toward shore, trying to figure a way of getting home.

Home Truths has a very different tone. Here is the blurb:

Home Truths

Bill Murphy spent a gruelling eight months examining a selection of English towns and cities and mixing with people whose way of life is football, the National Lottery, fly-on-the-wall documentaries and *Noel's House Party*. In *Home Truths*, an irreverent chronicle of his journey into the provinces, he paints a dark, wry picture of England today. Murphy certainly pulls no punches, and his portrayal of England's decaying society is guaranteed to provoke heated discussion.

The ending of *Home Truths* does not sum up the book in any way. However, you can get a clear idea of the tone from some of the chapter headings. Here are some of them!

1 Braintree – the ugliest collection of people in the UK outside Wales.
2 Southport – so dead, not even the sea turns up anymore.
3 Woking – built to service the Brookwood cemetery.
4 Slough – there are some places which have always been dreadful. Slough is one of them.

... and so it goes on!

So you can see that travel writing offers a wealth of material for linking and contrasting.

Same place – different time

ACTIVITY 31

Different travel writers choose different places to write about. For example, Murphy chose more obscure places, Bryson chose places he had visited before. If you want another dimension to compare, you can look at where the writers have in fact been to the same places. Defoe and Bryson both visited Salisbury – 270 years apart.

Bryson and Defoe both make comments on the Cathedral and its surroundings. Compare the methods by which each writer makes his feelings clear to the reader. You should look at the following aspects and support your comments with quotations:

- critical comments
- complimentary comments
- focus of attention (the actual topics the writer comments on)
- evidence each writer uses
- attitude of each writer to the place
- amount of knowledge each writer has.

Which extract would make you want to visit Salisbury?

Defoe writes:

The city of Salisbury has two remarkable manufactures carried on in it, and which employ the poor of great part of the country round; namely, fine flannels, and long cloths for the Turkey trade, called Salisbury Whites: the people of Salisbury are gay and rich, and have a flourishing trade; and there is a great deal of good manners and good company among them; I mean among the citizens, beside what is found among the gentlemen; for there are many good families in Salisbury, beside the citizens.

The city has a great addition from the Close, that is to say the circle of ground wall'd in adjacent to the Cathedral; in which the families of the prebendaries and commons, and others of the clergy belonging to the cathedral have their houses, as is usual in all cities where there are cathedral churches. These are so considerable here, and the place so large, that it is (as it is call'd in general) like another city.

The cathedral is famous for its spire, which is without exception the highest, and the handsomest in England, being from the ground 400 foot, and yet the walls so exceedingly thin, that at the upper part of the spire upon a view made by the late Christopher Wren, the wall was found to be less than five inches thick; upon which consultation was had, whether the spire, or at least the upper part of it should be taken down, it being supposed to have received some damage by the great storm in the year 1703; but it was resolv'd in the negative, and Sir Christopher order'd it to be strengthened with bands of iron plates, as has effectually secur'd it; and I have heard some of the best architects say, it is stronger now than when it was first built.

They tell us here long stories of the great art us'd in laying the first foundations of this great church; the ground being marshy and wet, occasion'd by the channels of the rivers, that it was laid upon piles according to some, and upon woolpacks according to others; but this is not suppos'd by those who know, that the whole country is one rock of chalk, even from the tops of the highest hills, to the bottom of the deepest rivers.

They tell us the church was forty years a building, and cost an immense sum of money, but it must be acknowledged that the inside of the work is not answerable in the decoration of things, to the workmanship without: the painting in the choir is mean, and more like the ordinary method of common drawing room, or tavern painting, than that of a church; the carving is good but very little of it, and it is rather a fine church than finely set off.

Bryson writes:

Salisbury I must point out in all fairness, is actually much better at looking after itself than most other towns. Indeed it is the very handsomeness of the place generally makes the odd desecrations so difficult to bear. Moreover it appears little by little to be getting better. The local authority has recently insisted that a cinema owner preserve the half timbered façade on a sixteenth century building in the town centre and I noticed two places where the developers appeared to be actually taking apart buildings that had been despoiled during the dark ages of the sixties and seventies and restoring them with diligence and care. One of the developers boards boasted that it did this sort of thing more or less always. May it prosper for ever.

I would probably forgive Salisbury anything as long as they never mess with Cathedral Close. There is no doubt in my mind that Salisbury Cathedral is the single most beautiful structure in England and the close around it the most beautiful space. Every stone, every wall, every shrub is just right. It is as if every person who has touched if for 700 years has only improved it. I could live on a bench in the grounds. I sat on one now and gazed happily for half an hour at this exquisite composition of cathedral, lawns and solemn houses. I'd have stayed longer except that it started to drizzle . . .

I wandered across the broad lawn to the cathedral. In the tragic event that you have never been there, I warn you now that Salisbury has long been the most money-keen of English cathedrals . . . Salisbury takes things a good step beyond what I would call discreet solicitation.

First you have to pass a cinema-style ticket booth where you are encouraged to pay a voluntary admission charge of £2.50, then once inside you are repeatedly assaulted with further calls on your pocket. You are asked to pay to hear a recorded message or make a brass rubbing, to show your support for the Salisbury Cathedral Girl Choristers and the Friends of Salisbury Cathedral, and to help restore something called the Eisenhower flag, a seriously faded and tattered Stars and Stripes that once hung in Eisenhower's command post at Wilton House near by. (I left 10p and a note saying: 'But why did you let it get in such a state in the first place?'). Altogether, I counted nine separate types of contributions box between the admission booth and the gift shop – ten if you include the one for votive candles. On top of that, you could hardly move through the nave without bumping into an upright display introducing the cathedral staff (there were smiling photographs of each of them, as if this were Burger King) or discussing the church's Voluntary Work Overseas or glass cases with cutaway models showing you how the cathedral was constructed – diverting I grant you, but surely more appropriate to the museum across the close. It was a mess. How long I wonder, till you climb into an electric cart and are whirred through the 'Salisbury Cathedral Experience' complete with animatronic stonemasons and monks like Friar Tuck? I give it five years.

In this chapter we have examined the concept of genre. You have seen examples of texts which can be compared because they are in the same genre and you have had the chance to do some comparing yourself. We have taken a closer look at the genres of *bildungsroman*, autobiography and travel writing.

Your genre filing cabinets may well need sorting out by now!

Answers to Activity 30:

Text A: *Broke through Britain*
Text B: *Notes From A Small Island*
Text C: *Kingdom by the Sea*

3 The Theme's the Thing

In this chapter you will look at how you can use theme as a way of comparing and linking texts. This is not perhaps as easy as it sounds! We really need to decide first of all what a *theme* is and how this differs from the *content* of the text. Basically the *content* of a text is what it is about when you read it for the first time (or when you read something for enjoyment and not for an English course!). The *theme* is what thoughts or issues the text evokes in you, how your experience relates to the text and what light the text sheds on real life and its trials and tribulations. In other words what you *learn* from what happens in the text. The theme is the abstract concept which underlies the text. The best literature can be read for its engaging story or content and also its thought-provoking themes.

Bangers and mash or chalk and cheese?

Consider why the words 'bangers and mash' go together. Now consider why 'chalk and cheese' go together.

It is fairly obvious that 'bangers and mash' are paired because they are both types of food and they are usually eaten together. This is the 'sameness' or similarity between the texts. 'Chalk and cheese', however, are put together because they are so different and the expression itself is used to indicate things that are wildly different. The actual words were probably paired for the simple reason that they begin with the same letters and have a pleasing sound. After that the comparison breaks down because the objects have nothing really in common. Comparing chalk and cheese is of little value because they are *too* different. There are obvious differences between 'bangers and mash' but there is a basis for comparison and some interesting remarks to be made about shape and texture. You could say that 'bangers and mash' have the same theme whereas the words 'chalk and cheese' look similar and sound similar but the objects the words represent are very different indeed. Chalk and cheese also have very different purposes of course!

Sweetcorn and maize? These objects look very much alike but on investigation you would find one rather nice to eat and the other unpalatable. Maize is the generic name for a cereal plant which is usually grown for animal feed. Sweetcorn is a specific type of maize which has sweet kernels and is eaten by us as a vegetable. It is difficult to distinguish between these two items without a very close visual examination or by tasting them. These two items are the equivalent of literature where the end product looks at first glance to be identical but their purposes are different. Pope's mock epic *The Rape of the Lock* could be compared to Milton's *Paradise Lost* on this basis as could particular poems in Blake's *Songs of Innocence and Experience*.

Enough of this culinary imagery. Let's get down to some definitions. The content of a text is what it is about at a story level – that is, what actually happens.

The theme of a text is its central idea or message – what the writer is trying to say to us through the text. This can be demonstrated by looking at the way the text is written as well as what actually happens. Many aspects of the text suggest its theme as well as its story line.

ACTIVITY 32

1 Study the following poem by Philip Larkin. The title has been omitted. When you have read it a few times write down a title which you think would be suitable. Bear in mind that this chapter is looking at themes so you should give the title some consideration and try, if you can, to indicate what you think the theme of the poem might be. It is unlikely you will come up with the same title as Larkin did, but you might come up with something equally appropriate.

2 Write a sentence stating the content of the poem. Now write a sentence outlining its theme. Make a list of quotations from the poem to show how you arrived at your theme.

The eye can hardly pick them out
From the cold shade they shelter in,
Till the wind distresses tail and mane;
Then one crops grass, and moves about
– The other seeming to look on –
And stands anonymous again.

Yet fifteen years ago, perhaps
Two dozen distances sufficed
To fable them; faint afternoons
Of Cups and Stakes and Handicaps,
Whereby their names were artificed
To inlay faded, classic Junes –

Silks at the start: against the sky
Numbers and parasols: outside,
Squadrons of empty cars, and heat,
And littered grass: then the long cry
Hanging unhushed till it subsides
To stop-press columns on the street.

Do memories plague their ears like flies?
They shake their heads. Dusk brims the shadows.
Summer by summer all stole away,
The starting-gates, the crowd and cries –
All but the unmolesting meadows.
Almanacked, their names live; they

Have slipped their names, and stand at ease,
Or gallop for what must be joy,

And not a field glass sees them home.
Or curious stopwatch prophesies:
Only the groom, and the groom's boy,
With bridles in the evening come.

3 Find out the original title for yourself and notice its metaphorical significance. The poem is about horses. Hopefully you will have also come up with its theme which will be revealed quite clearly when you discover the original title. The answer is given at the end of this chapter.

ACTIVITY 33

Another horsy tale

1 Below is a poem by Edwin Muir called *The Horses*. You will have guessed what its content is by its title. Study it and be prepared to give an opinion on the following aspects.

■ When do you think the poem is set?

■ Can you find any biblical imagery?
■ Pick out any particularly striking images and comment on them.
■ Look at the break in the text and suggest why it is there and what its effect is.
■ Pick out all the words used to describe these 'strange horses.'

The Horses

Barely a twelvemonth after
The seven days war that put the world to sleep,
Late in the evening the strange horses came.
By then we had made our covenant with silence,
But in the first few days it was so still
We listened to our breathing and were afraid.
On the second day
The radios failed; we turned the knobs; no answer.
On the third day a warship passed us, heading north,
Dead bodies piled on the deck. On the sixth day
A plane plunged over us into the sea. Thereafter
Nothing. The radios dumb;
And still they stand in corners of our kitchens,
And stand, perhaps, turned on, in a million rooms
All over the world. But now if they should speak,
If on a sudden they should speak again,
If on the stroke of noon a voice should speak,
We would not listen, we would not let it bring
That old bad world that swallowed its children quick
At one great gulp. We would not have it again.
Sometimes we think of the nations lying asleep,
Curled blindly in impenetrable sorrow,
And then the thought confounds us with its strangeness.
The tractors lie about our fields; at evening
They look like dank sea-monsters couched and waiting.
We leave them where they are and let them rust:
'They'll moulder away and be like other loam.'
We make our oxen drag our rusty ploughs,
Long laid aside. We have gone back
Far past our fathers' land.
                    And then, that evening

Late in the summer the strange horses came.
We heard a distant tapping on the road,
A deepening drumming; it stopped, went on again
And at the corner changed to hollow thunder.
We saw the heads
Like a wild wave charging and were afraid.
We had sold our horses in our fathers' time
To buy new tractors. Now they were strange to us
As fabulous steeds set on an ancient shield
Or illustrations in a book of knights.
We did not dare go near them. Yet they waited,
Stubborn and shy, as if they had been sent
By an old command to find our whereabouts
And that long-lost archaic companionship.
In the first moment we had never a thought
That they were creatures to be owned and used.
Among them were some half-a-dozen colts
Dropped in some wilderness of the broken world,
Yet new as if they had come from their own Eden.
Since then they have pulled our ploughs and borne our loads,
But that free servitude still can pierce our hearts.
Our life is changed; their coming our beginning.

2 Read the whole poem again in the light of what you have discovered so far from tackling the questions.
3 Now write a sentence to outline its theme.

Share this as a group. You may be able to come up with an alternative title which would indicate more about the theme of the poem.

ACTIVITY 34

So what?

So we have looked at two poems which are, on the surface, about horses. In fact neither of them is primarily about simple straightforward horses. Probably the only similarity between these two poems is their basic subject matter. Discuss if you think there is much to be gained from a detailed comparison of these two poems.

You may come up with the idea that in fact all you can do is look at their differences which may not be a particularly subtle way of progressing. Chalk and cheese! However, you might think that a detailed study of the poetic techniques of these poems would form the basis of a knowledgeable and worthwhile comparison: 'bangers and mash'.

ACTIVITY 35

Make a list of all the texts you have studied in your study of English at GCSE, AS or A2 level. For each one write an outline of *either* its theme *or* its content. Swap your outlines with other students. Try to decide if you have been given a 'content' or a 'theme'. If you know the text you have been given try to provide an outline of its

theme or content (the one you have not been given!). You should now have a selection of texts with their theme and contents outlined. See if any of these texts can be linked. If you can, choose two and make a chart of their similarities and differences taking into account what you have learned so far.

Paperback pairings

The covers of paperback books are useful
resources. These three novels about people on a
desert island are frequently quoted as having the
same content.

Discuss the front covers of these novels and
suggest what the themes may be just by
examining in detail what is portrayed on the
cover. You may already know some of them.

The novels are *Robinson Crusoe* by Daniel Defoe,
Lord of the Flies by William Golding and *The
Beach* by Alex Garland. (There is more discussion
of *The Beach* and *Lord of the Flies* in Chapter 5.)

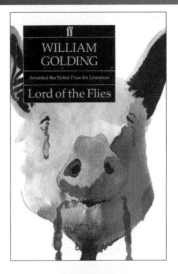

The picture of Robinson Crusoe shows he has taken advantage of the
natural things on the island as well as the items he salvaged. He has used
his initiative and looks comfortable and competent! Perhaps this is not
really a true picture of life on a desert island. Crusoe is definitely a survivor.

The pig's head dripping with blood suggests that the inhabitants of the island have managed to provide themselves with food but at the same time it demonstrates their descent into savagery. The blood dripping from the eye is like a tear. It is an uncomfortable picture which disturbs the onlooker.

The human eye staring from the cover of *The Beach* is also disturbing. It is piercing and suggests introspection. The footmarks leading to it are like tears. The outline of a coast is idyllic but the superimposed eye is disconcerting to say the least.

ACTIVITY 37

Here are some comments on each of these texts. Identify which text is being discussed. See if you can add the correct year of publication (1954, 1719, 1996).

The answers are at the end of the chapter.

Text A

This is a book about a group of people on an island which seems like paradise. Left to their own devices the group disintegrates and gradually reverts to barbarity, savagery and murder.

Text B

This is a book which is mostly an adventure story. The intricate details give a sense of realism but it has no real psychological depth. The native of the island is treated as a servant.

Text C

This book is a landmark in a genre classified as imaginative travel writing. It is about back-packers looking for paradise. It is a journey into the unknown. It is a well documented adventure story.

These three books provide an excellent selection to link. We have started the process here from simply examining the covers and some very basic information about each text.

Variations on a theme

There are only a limited number of themes but there are lots of possible variations on a theme.

A very common theme is boy meets girl, loses girl, finds another, realises he wants the first, finds the first again etc. ... but there is more to literature than this very common, if intriguing, story line.

ACTIVITY 38

Make a list of texts you know well and try to summarise the basic theme. Use the material from the previous activity if you like. Boy meets girl may be one. Persecution may be another. Perhaps you will find a text about the development of self knowledge, a text which questions the nature of mankind, one which simply shows how we cannot escape our destiny, or one which shows man's inhumanity to man. From this activity make a list of very broad themes. Try to make the list as short as you can by using the idea of variations on a theme and refining the theme to its really basic idea.

Here is a list of some common themes in prose. They may be similar to your list but there may be differences. This is perfectly acceptable – in fact it's a good thing!

- Boy meets girl (love)
- The development of the life and personality of a character influenced by events and other people
- Isolation of an individual or a group and its effects
- Utopias/dystopias (an imaginary place where everything is as bad or as good as it could possibly be)
- Ways of surviving
- Justice/injustice/fate
- Women's struggle
- Rejection/prejudice
- Man's inhumanity to man.

Add any broad themes that you discovered which are not mentioned here. Argue the case for their inclusion.

Consider this list of novels and see if you know, or can find out, which theme they fit into most comfortably. You could find copies of the texts and look at the blurb or look on the Internet for a synopsis. Be prepared to argue your case!

- *Lord of the Flies*
- *The Handmaid's Tale*
- *Tess of the D'Urbervilles*
- *Romeo and Juliet*
- *Nineteen Eighty-Four*
- *Great Expectations*
- *To Kill a Mocking Bird*
- *Snow Falling on Cedars*
- *I Know Why the Caged Bird Sings*
- *Pride and Prejudice*
- *Wuthering Heights*
- *The Catcher in the Rye.*

There are also texts on the subject of human nature – in particular its frailty. Many of Shakespeare's plays have themes along these lines. Can you name any plays by Shakespeare which deal with jealousy, pride, ambition, greed?

It is not possible or even beneficial to look at all of these themes here, but we can look in detail at a few and suggest some ideas about what sort of links there are between different texts with the same theme and how to tackle exploring these.

Man's inhumanity to man

Let's look at two texts which show us something about the nature of mankind. They are rather depressing accounts of colonisation and its effects – the play, *The Royal Hunt of the Sun* by Peter Shaffer which was first performed in 1964, and the novel, *Things Fall Apart* by Chinua Achebe published in 1958, will form the basis of this discussion.

Chinua Achebe's novel establishes the Nigerian community in all its complexity and humanity and then shows how the white man assumes the native people are savages. The novel is set at the end of the nineteenth century. The white man proceeds to destroy the civilisation which the reader has been closely involved with and has developed sympathy for. We have learnt about the system of justice, the marriage customs, the religion, the 'foreign policy', the family relationships and other age-old customs. This novel is narrated in the third person but the narrator seems to be a sympathetic 'elder' of the Nigerian people.

Shaffer's play is about the exploitation of Peru by the Spanish in the early sixteenth century and how the country was plundered for its gold under the guise of converting 'savages' to Christianity. The narrator in this play is one of the characters who, as a young man, was part of the army which exploited Peru.

Thus, the common theme is how one group of supposedly civilised people can impose its will on a group of people who are on the surface weaker and supposedly uncivilised. One of the authorial purposes is the same – to show man's inhumanity to man with particular reference to a clash of cultures.

The similarities centre around the theme, obviously, but it's worth looking at the differences early on to see if they affect the theme.

Differences

- Geographical setting – one is set in Africa, the other is in South America
- Genre – one is a novel, the other is a play
- Time – there is a time difference of two centuries in the setting
- How it is told – the narrator in the play is a character closely involved in the events but at a time later in his life when he can reflect on events. The narrator in the novel is almost like a sympathetic elder of the tribe telling the story – it has the feel of story telling about it.

ACTIVITY 41

Who are the authors?
It would be worth looking up some biographical information on these authors to see if the texts here are typical of the writings of the author. You could write a short biography of each to see what the similarities and differences are. This would give you a clear indication of where the authors are 'coming from' in terms of background and attitudes.

How do they feel about their subject?
If we look at a brief extract from each text we can establish something about the attitude of the authors to their subject. We can see how

sympathy is created by the writer for the indigenous (native) population.

A detailed look at specific sections.
So where do we start if we want to develop the links between these texts? We have established that the theme is fairly similar. We have established some basic differences. You would need to read the whole texts to get a clear idea of how the other themes are developed. However, here we can consider specific extracts from the texts to look at the author's treatment of the indigenous people.

At the end of *Things Fall Apart*, after the reader has been privy to the Nigerian society and its complexity, the white District Commissioner arrives and his treatment of the community is devastating. The final paragraph gives the reader a jolt and brings home 'man's inhumanity to man'.

> In the many years in which he [the Commissioner] had toiled to bring civilisation to different parts of Africa he had learnt a number of things. One of them was that a District Commissioner must never attend to such undignified details as cutting down a dead man from a tree. Such attention would give the natives a poor opinion of him. In the book which he planned to write he would stress that point. As he walked back to the court he thought about that book. Every day brought him some new material. The story of this man who had killed a messenger and hanged himself would make interesting reading. One could almost write a whole chapter on him. Perhaps not a whole chapter but a reasonable paragraph, at any rate. There was so much else to include, and one must be firm in cutting out details. He had already chosen the title of the book, after much thought: *The Pacification of the Primitive Tribes of the Lower Niger.*

And that's the end of the book!

Most readers are incensed when they see the main noble character, Okonkwo, relegated to the simple description of 'a dead man' who is worth perhaps 'a reasonable paragraph' in a book. We have just read a whole book which creates him as both a hero and a villain and this is what he is reduced to. He is worth more than a paragraph surely in any book – even this one!

The tribe are only interested in war when all else fails. They are willing to negotiate first. Much of the violence is provoked by the white man. The idea of the native people being made peaceful (pacification) is ironic.

The District Commissioner's character is made clear in this extract. He was too important to be bothered with the indignity of suicide. He had to remain aloof from the local people in case they got a 'poor opinion of him'. He had to be firm in his decisions at whatever level. The life and death of a man is reduced by him to 'interesting reading'.

Let's look at the beginning of the book to see how the author establishes the character of this dead man.

> Okonkwo was well known throughout the nine villages and even beyond. His fame rested on solid personal achievements. As a young man of eighteen he had brought honour to his village by throwing Amalinze the Cat. Amalinze was the great wrestler who for seven years was unbeaten from Umnofia to Mbaino.

> The drums beat and the flutes sang and the spectators held their breath. Amalinze was a wily craftsman, but Okonkwo was as slippery as a fish in water. Every nerve and every muscle stood out on their arms, on their backs and their thighs, and one almost heard them stretching to breaking point. In the end Okonkwo threw the Cat ... He was tall and huge, and his bushy eyebrows and wide nose gave him a severe look. He breathed heavily, and it was said that, when he slept, his wives and children in their out houses could hear him breathe.

A fine strong man indeed. As the story progresses we see his faults and shortcomings but nevertheless he is a 'noble savage'. He is strong, successful and formidable. The physical description of him is graphic. He is awesome! During the story Okonkwo watches as members of his tribe are worn down and dispossessed by the colonisers. The book is about one noble man's struggle against oppression by a supposedly superior race – 'man's inhumanity to man'.

The beginning of *The Royal Hunt of the Sun* sets the scene for the distressing way in which the Incas in Peru were treated by their invaders.

The narrator, Old Martin, begins by talking about his leader Francisco Pizarro, the Spaniard who invaded Peru. He is the equivalent figure to the District Commissioner in that he is responsible for the treatment of the indigenous people and is seen as unworthy himself. Old Martin says:

Soon I'll be dead and they'll bury me out here in Peru, the land I helped ruin as a boy. This story is about ruin. Ruin and gold ... I'm going to tell you how one hundred and sixty-seven men conquered an empire of twenty-four million. And then things that no-one has ever been told: things to make you groan and cry out I'm lying ... If you could only imagine what it was like for me at the beginning to be allowed to serve him. But boys don't dream like that any more – service! Conquest! Riding down Indians in the name of Spain. The inside of my head was one vast plain for feats of daring ...

The great conqueror then is not all he seems to be. What then of the indigenous people, the Incas? The Inca civilisation is one of the great marvels of the world. Their buildings still stand over four hundred years later. Their communication system was incredible. Their artistry is mind boggling! In the play the Inca leader is Atahuallpa. Here is an extract from the beginning of the play when Atahuallpa is introduced:

The stage darkens and the huge medallion high on the back wall begins to glow. Great cries of Inca are heard ... Exotic music mixes with the chanting. Slowly the medallion opens outwards to form a huge golden sun with twelve great rays. In the centre stands Atahuallpa, sovereign Inca of Peru, masked, crowned and dressed in gold. When he speaks his voice like the voices of all the Incas, is strangely formalised.

This is the person who is ruined and degraded by the Spanish General Francisco Pizarro.

So, what have we done?

Once you have established the main similarities in theme of your texts, you can then start to examine them in detail. Here we looked at the portrayal of the native and the invader. In both cases the native is noble and worthy and the invader is ignoble and unworthy. Here is a concrete way in which you can demonstrate the way a theme is developed in two texts. You should choose two extracts which have the same purpose in the text and look at them in detail. This will enable you to understand and show how the writer creates an attitude in the reader and this helps to establish the theme. There is more discussion on style in the final chapter of this book.

Utopias and Dystopias

ACTIVITY 42

Now it's your turn!

Below is an extract from the beginning of *The Handmaid's Tale* by Margaret Atwood and *Nineteen Eighty-Four* by George Orwell. These texts examine what could happen in a future where the powerless are totally controlled by the powerful. They are interesting reading. Both have been made into feature films. *Nineteen Eighty-Four* was written in 1948 and *The Handmaid's Tale* was published in 1987. You might like to consider how far predictions of the future of the last century are coming true in this one!

If you have read these texts you will be able to write in general about the similarities in content and theme. Here you will be able to look at the beginning of them both and see how the writer sets the scene in order to develop his or her theme.

Read the extracts and then answer the questions at the end of the extracts.

Nineteen Eighty-Four

It was a bright cold day in April, and the clocks were striking thirteen. Winston Smith, his chin nuzzled into his breast in an effort to escape the vile wind, slipped quickly through the glass doors of Victory Mansions, though not quickly enough to prevent a swirl of gritty dust from entering along with him.

The hallway smelt of burnt cabbage and old rag mats. At one end of it a coloured poster, too large for indoor display, had been tacked to the wall. It depicted simply an enormous face, more than a metre wide: the face of a man of about forty-five, with a heavy black moustache and ruggedly handsome features. Winston made for the stairs. It was no use trying the lift. Even at the best of times it was seldom working, and at present the electric current was cut off during daylight hours. It was part of the economy drive in preparation for Hate Week. The flat was seven flights up, and Winston, who was thirty-nine and had a varicose ulcer above his right ankle, went slowly, resting several times on the way. On each landing, opposite the lift shaft, the poster with an enormous face gazed from the wall. It was one of those pictures which are so contrived that the eyes follow you about when you move. BIG BROTHER IS WATCHING YOU, the caption beneath it ran.

Inside the flat a fruity voice was reading out a list of figures which had something to do with the production of pig iron. The voice came from an oblong metal plaque like a dulled mirror which formed part of the surface of the right-hand wall. Winston turned a switch and the voice sank somewhat, though the words were distinguishable. The instrument (the telescreen as it was called) could be dimmed but there was no way of shutting it off completely. He moved over to the window: a smallish, frail figure, the meagreness of his body merely emphasised by the blue overalls which were the uniform of the Party. His hair was very fair, his face naturally sanguine, his skin roughened by coarse soap and blunt razor blades and the cold of the winter that had just ended.

The Handmaid's Tale

We slept in what had once been the gymnasium. The floor was of varnished wood, with stripes and circles painted on it, for the games that were formerly played there; the hoops for the basketball nets were still in place, though the nets were gone. A balcony ran around the room, for the spectators, and I thought I could smell, faintly like an afterimage, the pungent scent of sweat, shot through with the sweet taint of chewing gum and perfume from watching girls, felt skirted as I knew from the pictures, later in mini-skirts, then pants, then in one earring, spiky green-streaked hair. Dances would have been held there: the music lingered, a palimpsest of unheard sound, style upon style, an undercurrent of drums, a forlorn wail, garlands made of tissue paper flowers, cardboard devils, a revolving ball of mirrors, powdering the dancers with a snow of light . . .

We yearned for the future. How did we learn it, that talent for insatiability? It was in the air; and it was still in the air, an afterthought, as we tried to sleep, in the army cots that had been set up in rows so we could not talk. We had flannelette sheets, like children's and army issue blankets, old ones that still said U.S. We folded our clothes neatly and laid them on the stools at the end of the beds. The lights were turned down but not out. Aunt Sara and Aunt Elizabeth patrolled; they had electric cattle prods slung on thongs from their leather belts.

No guns though, even they could not be trusted with guns. Guns were for the guards, especially picked from the Angels. The guards weren't allowed inside the building except when called, and we weren't allowed out, except for our walks, twice daily, two by two around the football field which was enclosed now by a chain link fence topped with barbed wire.

- How is the atmosphere created? Look at appeals to the senses.
- What hints are there of the tone of the rest of each book?
- How and where do you get the feeling of repression?
- Who is telling the story and what is the effect of this? What don't you understand?

- What is familiar and what is unfamiliar about the settings?

There is much to be gained from a detailed study of the very beginning of texts that are linked.

Poetic themes

1 Individually, collect three anthologies of poetry. Use ones that arrange the poems in themes rather than in poets. List the themes that the editors have selected. As a group make a complete list of the themes that have occurred in your anthologies.
2 Compare your list with this one and name two poems for each theme:

- War (World War 1, World War 2, more recent wars)
- The natural world (animals, the seasons)
- Love/marriage
- Growing up/adolescence

- Family relationships
- Growing old/death/grief
- Present society and its problems.
- The future

These are probably the most popular themes for poetry. Many poems of course would combine some of these themes. Poems on love often have thoughts of death and grief in them. Growing up and family relationships are associated together. There are also more refined aspects of each of these themes. Love poems can be triumphant or despairing. Growing old can be a challenge or a chore.

ACTIVITY 44

In pairs, choose two poems you have already studied and write down in one sentence what the main theme is which links them. Now be more discriminating and discuss where the differences lie. You could refer back to the discussion on *Warning* by Jenny Joseph and *On Ageing* by Maya Angelou which are given in full in Chapter 1.

ACTIVITY 45

This is a class activity.

If it is practical, as an individual, provide two poems with two different but predictable themes from your chosen anthology. Divide into groups of four and distribute copies of all the poems to all the groups. The task is to put the poems into themes and justify your decision as a group to the others. Compare your classification with the other groups. There will be variation about the classification but this is fine if you can justify your choice.

Ashes to ashes

Death is something that we cannot escape. Let's look at two poems on the death of parents.

Long Distance

Though my mother was already two years dead
Dad kept her slippers warming by the gas
put hot water bottles her side of the bed
and still went to renew her transport pass.

You couldn't just drop in. You had to phone.
He'd put you off an hour to give him time
to clear away her things and look alone
as though his still raw love were such a crime.

He couldn't risk my blight of disbelief
though sure that very soon he'd hear her key
scrape in the rusted lock and end his grief.
He knew she'd just popped out to get the tea.

I believe that life ends with death, and that is all.
You haven't both gone shopping; just the same,
in my new black leather phone book there's your name
and the disconnected number I still call.

Tony Harrison

Dad

Your old hat hurts me, and those black
fat raisins you liked to press into
my palm from your soft heavy hand:
I see you staggering back up the path
with sacks of potatoes from some local farm,

fresh eggs, flowers. Every day I grieve
for your great heart broken and you gone.
You loved to watch the trees. This year
you did not see their Spring.
The sky was freezing over the fen
as on that somewhere secretly appointed day
you beached: cold white-faced, shivering.

What happened, old bull, my loyal
hoarse-voiced warrior? The hammer
blow that stopped you in your track
and brought you to a hospital monitor
could not destroy your courage
to the end you were
uncowed and unconcerned with pleasing anyone.

I think of you now as once again safely
at my mother's side, the earth as
chosen as a bed, and feel most sorrow for
all that was gentle in
my childhood buried there
already, forfeit, now forever lost.

Elaine Feinstein

COMMENTARY
In both of these poems a child is grieving for a parent. In the poem by
Harrison it seems as if the poet cannot understand the behaviour of his
father and also the father couldn't risk the poet's 'blight of disbelief'. The
poet knows that his father cannot accept his mother's death but sees it as
illogical 'as life ends with death and that is all'. The actions his father
performs to pretend his mother is still alive are gently tolerated. However,
after both parents are dead it seems that the poet himself has the same
attitude. Even in his new phone book he has their 'disconnected number'.
The poem is in a regular pattern with regular rhyme which implies that
nothing is changing. The final stanza, however, has a slightly different
rhyme scheme. Does this suggest a change in focus? The poet is now
echoing the actions of his father rather than commenting in disbelief on
those actions. Things have changed slightly.

Feinstein's poem mourns the loss of her father. There is no disbelief and
pretence here. The poet admits that she remembers her father everyday and
there is no denial. There is some detail about the manner of his death.
There is consolation in the idea that he is now 'at my mother's side' rather
than thinking he is still there to be visited. The stanza lengths are
consistent except the fourth one which is longer. This one deals with his
actual death and his strength and courage at the end. The poet wants to
dwell on this. The patterning in this poem is not in the rhyme at the end
of lines but in the sounds, for example 'fat' and 'black', 'uncowed' and
'unconcerned', and ideas – 'already forfeit, now forever lost'.

Notice that the poems are also about family relationships as well as death.

Growing old

1 Here are two poems on the theme of growing old. One deals with women and one with men. From the tone and content of these poems suggest something of the background of the poets and then look them up in an anthology to check your findings.

2 Examine the imagery in the first poem. What attitude to the old people does it show?

3 What are the old men thinking about in the second poem? How is this different from the thoughts of the old women?

Old Ladies Home

Sharded in black like beetles,
Frail as antique earthenware
One breath might shiver to bits,
The old women creep out here
To sun themselves on the rocks or prop
Themselves up against the wall
Whose stones keep a little heat.

Needles knit in bird-beaked
Counterpoint to their voices:
Sons, daughters, daughters and sons
Distant and cold as photos
Grandchildren nobody knows.
Age wears the best black fabric
Rust-red or green as lichens.

At owl call the old ghosts flock
To hustle them off the lawn.
From beds boxed-in like coffins
The bonneted ladies grin.
And death, that bald-head buzzard,
Stalls in halls where the lamp wick
Shortens with each breath drawn.

Sylvia Plath

Two Old Black Men on a Leicester Square Park Bench

What do you dream of you
old black men sitting
on park benches staunchly
wrapped up in scarves
and coats of silence
eyes far away from the cold
grey and strutting
pigeon
ashy fingers trembling
(though it's said that the old
hardly ever feel the cold)

do you dream revolutions
you could have forged
or mourn

some sunfull woman you might have known a
hibiscus flower
ghost memories of desire

O it's easy
to rainbow the past
after all the letters from
home spoke of hardships

and the sun was traded long ago

Grace Nichols

Growing up

ACTIVITY 47

Difficult students are the theme of these two poems. Read them carefully and identify the themes in each. Write a brief character sketch of each child using evidence from the poem to support your assertions.

A Difficult Child

More proficient than a ventriloquist,
he imitates birdcalls with a shut mouth;
with a conjurer's deftness, he can throw
balls of paper across the class without
moving his hands from the desk. He can spit
bubble-gum so high in the air that
it sticks to the ceiling. Whatever he
does, demands attention. Once he even
lit a cigarette, took a puff, and stubbed
it out in a sudden mime so swiftly
executed that he didn't seem to move
at all, and the whole class applauded him.
Chewing paper, he rolls it on his tongue
and shoots it right into the teacher's ear.
Twelve years age when chocolates were
rationed and flowers expensive, a young
man gave a girl this bastard. The teacher
wonders what use punishment would be for
one who has never known anything else.

Zulfikar Ghose

The Good Teachers

You run round the back to be in it again.
No bigger than your thumbs, those virtuous women
size you up from the front row. Soon now,
Miss Ross will take you for double History.
You breathe on the glass, making a ghost of her, say
South Sea Bubble Defenestration of Prague.

You love Miss Pirie. So much, you are top

of her class. So much, you need two of you
to stare out from the year, serious, passionate.
The River's Tale by Rudyard Kipling by heart.
Her kind intelligent green eye. Her cruel blue one.
You are making a poem up for her in your head.

But not Miss Sheridan. Comment vous appelez.
But not Miss Appleby. Equal to the square
of the other two sides. Never Miss Webb.
Dar es Salaam. Kilimanjaro. Look. The good teachers
swish down the corridor in long, brown skirts,
snobbish and proud and clean and qualified.

And they've got your number. You roll the waistband
of your skirt over and over, all leg, all
dumb insolence, smoke-rings. You won't pass.
You could do better. But there's the wall you climb
into dancing, lovebites, marriage, the Cheltenham
and Gloucester, today. The day you'll be sorry one day.

Carol Ann Duffy

Marriage

ACTIVITY 48

The two poems below are thematically linked. They are both by men, but notice the events are seen through a woman's eyes.

After studying these two poems, discuss the role of each woman in the marriage and comment on their social situations. When you have established this go on to look at each poem in detail.

Here are some ideas to start you off. *The Wife's Tale* relies a great deal on evoking the senses of sight, sound and touch. Although the wife left as she 'belonged no further to the work', she

seems contented with her position. Her care for the men seems appreciated.

The feeling in *Portrait of a Marriage* is quite different. Notice the negative words 'mild rebellion', 'insecurity', 'remorse', 'false' and the violence of 'the stabbed evenings'. What are the connotations of 'Joseph's coat'? What is the significance of the 'unlocked door'?

Continue your analysis until you feel you have really seen the similarities and differences between these two poems.

The Wife's Tale

When I had spread it all on linen cloth
Under the hedge, I called them over.
The hum and gulp of the thresher ran down
And the big belt slewed to a standstill, straw
hanging undelivered in the jaws.
There was such quiet that I heard their boots
Crunching the stubble twenty yards away.

He lay down and said 'Give these fellows theirs,
I'm in no hurry,' plucking grass in handfuls

And tossing it in the air. 'That looks well.'
(He nodded at my white cloth on the grass.)
'I declare a woman could lay out a field
Though boys like us have little call for cloths.'
He winked, then watched me as I poured a cup
And buttered the thick slices that he likes.
'It's threshing better than I thought, and mind
It's good clean seed. Away over there and look.'
Always this inspection has to be made
Even when I don't know what to look for.
But I ran my hand in the half filled bags as hard as shot,
Innumerable and cool. The bags gaped
Where the chutes ran back to the stilled drum
And forks were stuck as javelins might mark lost battlefields.
I moved between them back across the stubble.

They lay in the ring of their own crusts and dregs
Smoking and saying nothing. 'There's good yield,
Isn't there?' – as proud as if he were the land itself –
'Enough for crushing and for sowing both.'
And that was it. I'd come and he had shown me
So I belonged no further to the work.
I gathered up the cups and folded up the cloth
And went. But they still kept their ease
Spread out, unbuttoned, grateful, under the trees.

                                                                                        Seamus Heaney

Portrait of a Marriage

To the suburban house you return again
with a new hat and the stammering discourse
of mild rebellion. You dare not entertain
questions like – Can I start again? Seek divorce?
Because now, middle aged, you would gain
nothing but insecurity and remorse,
all the might-have-beens crying in the brain.

It was false even before the first caress
but how you strove to make it true,
fouling silence, talking louder to suppress
the lie that somehow grew and grew,
as you hid each new distress
behind the photograph of the smile and you
less than radiant in your wedding dress.

And, in the stabbed evenings, when the sun
died, by appointment, in its Joseph's coat,
you asked for help from that anyone
whose million edition pen could write
romantic novels to overcome
the truth of the lonely all about,
the taste of nothing on your tongue.

Now, one year's gone since your clumsy honeymoon
and he talks to you behind an unlocked door;
again your artificial smile alone
floats between the ceiling and the floor,

like some quiet heartbreak, almost to condone
what, after all, others too must slow endure
the clock, the unhappiness, the civilised bore.

Until those tamed voices in this tidy room
weirdly rise again to show
what is your and your husband's doom,
the dullness you should never know,
the silent piano in the gloom,
the cut-glass vase you endow
with flowers, to disguise this here and now.

Dannie Abse

In this chapter ways of comparing texts with a similar theme have been suggested. You should now have a lot of ideas about ways to proceed with a comparison. Remember that theme alone will not really be sufficient. The way the author treats that theme will be interesting but obviously other issues relating to style, form and structure need to be examined.

Answer to the question in Activity 32:

The original title of the poem by Philip Larkin is *At Grass*.

Answers to question in Activity 37:

- Text A is *Lord of the Flies*, published in 1954
- Text B is *Robinson Crusoe*, published in 1719
- Text C is *The Beach*, published in 1996.

4 Cultural Connections

Study these two poems and justify the assertion
that they are modern. Look at the topic, the
language and the form.

The Nurse of the Man in the Pink Pyjamas

She knows the shade
shape
and smell of the shit
the swab of the red clogged throat
the temperatures
of mouth
armpit
and arse-
hole
the yellows
bulging catheter bags under the bed
that chart the death she keeps from him
is reminded by the pink
white
and yellow flowers on the cabinet
of the blooms of phlegm
but it doesn't stop her
lifting the arms
legs
and penis
to flannel them softly
smoothing the brow
combing the long grey hair over the pillow.

Jeremy Hughes

Noun Phrases

We were doing noun phrases
Sir said,

and I was looking across at Anna.
He picked up the bin.

What's this?
A bin.

Then I noticed Andy balling her too.
What's it made of?

Metal.
He could have any girl

and he was playing for mine.
What colour is it?

Grey.
And I kept sneaking a look at her

between the board, Andy and Sir.
What shape is it?

Square.
And then I saw her eyeing Andy

and my guts went.
The adjectives premodify the noun

Sir said,
now write four examples of your own.

The pretty girl.
The quiet boy.

The ignorant man.
The handsome bastard.

Jeremy Hughes

COMMENTARY These poems were written by a teacher and published in 2000. They would be difficult to place in any other era! The form is unusual and some of the language is colloquial or vulgar.

Noun Phrases demonstrates how a student can appear to be listening intently but is really thinking of something entirely different. Notice how, after the first question and answer, the question and reply are detached from each other. They are unconnected and irrelevant. The lines describing the behaviour of the girl and Andy thread through the poem. The important things are the thoughts about the girl and her relationship with the speaker and the 'handsome bastard', Andy. These thoughts interrupt the question and answer session. '(Eye)balling', 'sneaking', 'guts' are the language of school boys. The subject is love and jealousy – a perennial theme.

The first poem is a rather vivid description of an old man in a hospital which leaves little to the imagination. The 'bulging catheter bags', 'the swab of the red clogged throat', 'the blooms of phlegm' describe vividly the bodily functions of the patient. The nurse, however, washes the man softly, smoothes his brow and combs the long grey hair. The subject is not about growing old but the 'death she keeps from him'. Keeping the patient alive and avoiding death is one of the main objects of the nurse.

The subject matter of these poems is conventional but the treatment is not. The poems are products of the cultural background of the new millennium.

We are all products of our background – both our personal background and the context in which we live. Also remember that some issues are going to be universal no matter what the cultural background of the writer or a text may be. In this chapter we shall be looking at three particular aspects. We shall examine poetry about war in different cultural situations. We shall be looking at the position of women in a variety of historical settings and then considering the cultural background of one minority group, black women, and how that affects and links their writing.

Literature reflects or pre-dates many cultural changes. Great literature is the product of an individual's mind and an individual's experience. It is not simply a reflection of the times of the writer although the time influences the work. You should not assume that the cultural background of writers makes their writing the same. Writers will be influenced by culture but not slaves to it.

What do we mean by culture?

Culture covers the beliefs, traditions, technology, behaviour, as well as the artistic and intellectual achievement of an era. You probably understand the idea of pop culture or youth culture. Culture also covers the entertainment of an era and its primary moral values. Culture changes with time. We now seem to be in a culture where we have to be constantly 'in touch' by means of mobile phones or the internet. Information is transmitted at an alarming rate. We also live in a time when international travel or backpacking is part of most young people's life plan. During the last century we have been through a culture of peace and a culture of protest.

Studying the cultural context of a text is an extension of studying the context of writing of the text with which you are already familiar.

The particular cultural connections covered in this chapter are:

- aspects of war and the effect the cultural climate has on the literature written
- the cultural aspects of the role of women, particularly with regard to marriage
- the cultural issues at work in literature written by black women.

Words of war

The involvement of a country in war, whether civil or between countries, is obviously an emotional issue. The attitudes towards such an activity vary from patriotism to terror to total rejection depending on the involvement of the writer and the cultural attitudes of the time. Literature about war can be written by the soldiers, by the leaders, by the injured, by the people left at home. It can cover recruitment, engagement, injury, convalescence, recovery and return to normality. It can be in the form of poetry, prose, fiction or non-fiction and be written by women or men. Here we are going to look at war literature in the light of its cultural background and begin to look at how literature about war varies with the cultural climate in which it is written.

Sacrifice, cynicism, heroism and horror

War arouses some kind of emotion in everyone. The obvious ones are patriotism and self-sacrifice for the good of one's country but also there can be revulsion at the thought of bloodshed and the unnecessary death of soldiers and ordinary citizens. Here are two poems written in different times from very different viewpoints.

The Battlefield

They dropped like flakes, they dropped like stars,
Like petals from a rose,
When suddenly across the June
A wind with fingers goes.

They perished in the seamless grass, –
No eye could find the place;
But God on his repealles list
Can summon every face.

Emily Dickinson

Jeux d'Enfants

Hush-a-bye, baby, on the tree top,
When the winds change the fall-out may stop;
When the truce breaks the napalm will fall;
Up will go baby, grannie and all.
Little Bo-Peep has lost her sheep,
And can't tell where to find them;
None will survive, and if she's alive
Her future trails behind them.
Little boy Blue heard Gabriel's horn;
There's blood in the meadow and fire in the corn.
Where are the boys who followed the sheep?
They're under the haycock, buried deep.
  See-saw, marching to war,
  Neutrons will be our new masters;
  There will be but the devil to pay
  Because of Atomic Disasters.
    Little Jack Horner
    Flat in a corner
    Under a mushroom sky;
    He bites on his thumb,
    Is sightless and numb
    And praying 'Please God let me die'
    Little Miss Muffet
    Now has to rough it,
    Eating her heart away;
    With no-one beside her,

Mutation inside her
Has frightened survivors away.
'Bye, Baby Bunting,
Submarines are hunting.
Please inform our next of kin
We tracked the guided missiles in.
　Ring-a-ring o' roses,
　The final chapter closes.
　I KISS you – I'll MISS you.
　All fall down

S. Russell Jones

COMMENTARY These poems were obviously written in different centuries, the nineteenth and the twentieth. The imagery of 'flakes', 'stars', 'petals' in the first poem obviously indicates the attitude to the deaths of these soldiers. The sacrifice is gentle, beautiful and natural. The Grim Reaper, who may have figured in a poem about death, is replaced by the personification of the wind with gentle fingers gathering the dead. There is the statement that God knows every face of every person. The simple rhyme scheme echoes the simple acceptance of the situation. It is a comforting poem.

Not so the second poem. This is most uncomfortable. It uses echoes of children's nursery rhymes to highlight the devastation of modern warfare. The words are familiar to us but in a slightly different form. The differences shock us. Perhaps Little Jack Horner 'sightless and numb' and Little Miss Muffet with 'mutation inside her' are the most poignant images in this poem. Notice how we feel almost like smiling because of the familiarity of the words. The changes made, however, create a tension between what we anticipate and what we actually read. This is a war of the future that would affect all people both born and unborn. Hopefully the threat of this type of war has passed but it was certainly a central issue in the second half of the twentieth century.

ACTIVITY 50

Here are the approximate dates of some of the wars or threats of wars during the twentieth century.

- 1914–1918
- 1939–1945
- Vietnam 1960–1989
- Threat of Nuclear War 1945–89

- Falklands 1982
- Ireland 1960s onwards

Match these dates with the poems below and justify your decision. Try to show the cultural differences in the approach of the poets. The answers are at the end of the chapter.

Text A

My Family

Did you see us on the telly, Mum?
When we all sailed away –
Laughing, waving, cheering
Like in the films of yesterday.

Did you read it in *The Sun*, Pop?

How we pasted them first time.
You told me all about your war,
What do you think of mine?

Did you get the letters home, dear?
How I missed you and was sad.
Did you give my love to Tracy?
Does she miss her funny Dad?

Did you see us on the hillside?
Could you spot which one was me?
Were the flowers very heavy
For a grown-up girl of three?

Text B

The Letter

With *BEF June 10. Dear Wife,
(O blast this pencil. 'Ere, Bill, lend's a knife.)
I'm in the pink at present dear.
I think the war will end this year.
We don't see much of them square-'eaded 'uns.
We're out of harm's way, not bad fed.
I'm longing for a taste of your old buns.
(Say, Jimmie, spare's a bite of bread.)
There don't seem much to say right now.
(Yer what? Then don't yer ruddy cow!
And give us back me cigarette!)
I'll soon be 'ome. You mustn't fret.
My feet's improvin', as I told you of.
We're out in rest now. Never fear.
(VRACH! By crumbs, but that was near.)
Mother might spare you half a sov.
Kiss Nell and Bert. When me and you –
(Eh? What the 'ell! Stand to? Stand to!
Jim, give's a hand with pack on, lad.
Guh! Christ I'm hit. Take 'old. Aye, bad.
No, damn your iodine. Jim? 'Ere!
Write my old girl, Jim, there's a dear.)

*British Expeditionary Forces

Text C

What Were They Like?

(1) Did the people of Vietnam
    use lanterns of stone?
(2) Did they hold ceremonies
    to reverence the opening of buds?
(3) Were they inclined to quiet laughter?
(4) Did they use bone and ivory,
    jade and silver for ornament?
(5) Had they an epic poem?
(6) Did they distinguish between speech and singing?
(1) Sir, their light hearts turned to stone.

It is not remembered whether in gardens
stone lanterns illuminated pleasant ways.
(2) Perhaps they gathered once to delight in blossom,
but after the children were killed
there were no more buds.
(3) Sir, laughter is bitter to the burned mouth.
(4) A dream ago, perhaps. Ornament is for joy.
All bones were charred.
(5) It is not remembered. Remember,
most were peasants; their life
was in rice and bamboo.
When peaceful clouds were reflected in the paddies
and the water buffalo stepped surely along the terraces,
maybe fathers told their sons old tales.
When bombs smashed those mirrors
there was time only to scream.
(6) There is an echo yet
of their speech which was like song.
It was reported their singing resembled
the flight of moths in the moonlight.
Who can say? It is silent now.

Text D

Air Raid

'Aircraft! Stand still you bloody fool.'
Too late. He's seen the movement and the glittering sun.
The Messerschmidt swoops down with flame-tipped guns.
Around your sprawling form the deadly bullets splatter,
And the lying tense fearful of the hideous chatter,
You feel Death's haunting figure stalking near,
Sweat, cold about your body, tingling with fear.

And now the plane has turned to its patrol.
You rise and fingers trembling light a cigarette,
One man lies groaning, arm smashed by a cannon-shell.
You pad a splint and bandage the jagged hole;
Now for the morphine, tell him not to fret,
He's bloody lucky he got off so well.

Text E (an extract)
YOUR ATTENTION, PLEASE –
The Polar DEW has just warned that
A nuclear rocket strike of
At least one thousand megatons
Has been launched by the enemy
Directly at our major cities.
This announcement will take
Two and a quarter minutes to make,
You therefore have a further
Eight and a quarter minutes
To comply with the shelter
Requirements published in the Civil
Defence Code – section Atomic Attack.

A specially shortened Mass
Will be broadcast at the end
Of this announcement –
Protestant and Jewish services
Will begin simultaneously –
Select your wavelength immediately
According to instructions
In the Defence Code. Do not
Take well-loved pets (including birds)
Into your shelter – they will consume
Fresh air. Leave the old and bed-
Ridden, you can do nothing for them.
Remember to press the sealing
Switch when everyone is in
The shelter. Set the radiation
Aerial, turn on the geiger barometer.
Turn off your television now.
Turn off your radio immediately
The services end. At the same time
Secure explosion plugs in the ears
Of each member of your family. Take
Down your Plasma flasks . . .

Text F

The Identification

So you think it's Stephen?
Then I'd best make sure
Be on the safe side as it were.
Ah, there's been a mistake. The hair
you see, it's black, now Stephen's fair . . .
What's that? The explosion?
Of course burnt black. Silly of me.
I should have known. Then let's get on.

The face, is that the face I ask?
That mask of charred wood
blistered, scarred could
that have been a child's face?
The sweater, where intact, looks
in fact all too familiar.
But one must be sure.

The scoutbelt. Yes that's his.
I recognise the studs he hammered in
not a week ago. At the age
when boys get clothes-conscious
now you know. It's almost
certainly Stephen. But one must
be sure. Remove all trace of doubt.
Pull out every splinter of hope.

Pockets. Empty the pockets
Handkerchief? Could be any schoolboy's.
Dirty enough. Cigarettes?

Oh this can't be Stephen.
I don't allow him to smoke you see.
He wouldn't disobey me. Not his father.
But that's his penknife. That's his alright.
And that's his key on the keyring
Gran gave him just the other night.
So this must be him.

I think I know what happened
... about the cigarettes
No doubt he was minding them
for one of the older boys.
Yes that's it.
That's him.
That's our Stephen.

COMMENTARY

These poems are all poignant and disturbing. Two in particular, *What Were They Like?* and *The Identification* show how war devastates the civilian population. These two could be linked because of their unusual presentation of the effects of war on an innocent population. Both poems suggest what has been lost during the conflict. The comparison between the time before and after the conflict is distressing.

In *What Were They Like?* the blunt questions in the first section seem to ask about a civilisation that has been lost and become part of history. It seems an impersonal set of questions to gain information. The replies to these questions suggest the difference between the situation before the war and afterwards. In each of the first five responses there is a contrast between the past and present. The semantic field of peace and pleasure created by 'light hearts', 'pleasant ways', 'delight', 'laughter', 'dream', 'ornament', 'peaceful', is destroyed in each response by 'hearts turned to stone', 'killed', 'bitter', 'charred', 'smashed', 'scream'. The final answer is like a dream itself with the suggestion that 'their singing resembled the flight of moths in the moonlight'. However, it is now gone forever. Notice how the image of moths shows the vulnerability of the people. The use of the passive voice in the impersonal 'It is not remembered' implies the detached attitude of the speaker but raises the emotion of the reader. 'It is silent now' shows the finality of the destruction. The war in Vietnam was a very controversial activity both in the United States and elsewhere. The devastation caused and the deaths of soldiers and civilians was considered to be unjustifiable.

The Identification shows the struggle of a family to come to terms with the death of their son. The repetition of the need to 'make sure' and be 'on the safe side' shows their hope against hope that there has been a mistake. The parent tries to make light of the situation in 'Silly of me' and the handkerchief that 'Could be any school boy's/Dirty enough'. The hair 'burnt black' and 'That mask of charred wood blistered, scarred' which used to be a face are particularly vivid. There is agony in the metaphor 'Pull out every splinter of hope'. Notice the pathos in the need to find a good reason for the cigarettes in his pocket. The use of the first person in this poem obviously increases its impact. The death of innocent young bystanders is an unnecessary and inevitable consequence of civil war.

ACTIVITY 51

Choose two other poems from the selection printed above and link them for content and style. Look at the aspects from which the events are related and the impact this has on the content. Discuss any particular aspects of the style which are interesting or unusual.

ACTIVITY 52

Find a war poem written from each of the following angles and list the effect of the attitude and perspective on the style and presentation of the poem. Many anthologies have poetry divided into sections which will help. Simon Fuller's collection *The Poetry of War* published by Longman for the BBC has a wide selection of poetry from different wars and different perspectives.

- A woman's point of view
- Recruitment
- Injury
- Recovery
- Looking back

If you are investigating the cultural aspects of war you can also read *Goodbye to All That* which is the autobiography of Robert Graves published in 1929 and the excellent trilogy by Sebastian Faulks *The Girl at the Lion d'Or*, *Birdsong* and *Charlotte Gray*. There is also the play, *Journey's End* written in 1928 by R.C. Sherriff which is set in the trenches of World War One.

Women's rights

Cultural attitudes to women writers, marriage and the position of women have changed with time and social conditions. Until fairly recently women writers found it difficult to write about the thoughts and feelings particular to women. With the rise of equal opportunities and equal pay, the development of reliable contraception, equality in education and a release of women from hard, time-consuming domestic chores by modern appliances, women have made some headway into a male dominated society. In January 2001, according to *The Sunday Times* bestsellers' list, half of the best-selling fiction books were written by women.

ACTIVITY 53

Can you name any Elizabethan women writers? Do some research to establish the names of the first women who made their mark in literary activity. Any history of English literature will provide the information. From the information you have collected, deduce when women had any sort of respectability as writers.

ACTIVITY 54

Men writing about women
Discuss if you think men can adequately portray the feelings of women in their writing and find some examples. D.H. Lawrence is a good example to start you off. There are two poems earlier in this chapter written by men but from a female perspective. See if you could have deduced this from the poems.

Some of the first literary pieces to establish the role of women were the sonnets of the Italian poet, Petrarch. He wrote a sonnet sequence in the fourteenth century to his beloved Laura. Their love was idealised by the poet and not reciprocated by Laura. This form was imitated in Elizabethan times by Sidney (*Astrophel and Stella* in 1591), Spenser (*Amoretti* in 1595) and Shakespeare who all wrote sonnet sequences which seemed to idealise women. Poems by men about women were more prevalent then women writing about themselves or their relationship with men.

However, there are some early poems about women's love for men and here is one written in the seventeenth century by Anne Bradstreet.

To My Dear and Loving Husband

If ever two were one, then surely we.
If ever man were loved by wife, then thee;
If ever wife was happy in a man,
Compare with me ye women if you can.
I prize thy love more than whole mines of gold.
Or all the riches that the East doth hold.
My love is such that rivers cannot quench,
Nor aught but love from thee, give recompence.
Thy love is such I can no way repay,
The heavens reward thee manifold I pray.
Then while we live, in love let's so persever,
That when we live no more, we may live for ever.

This poem is similar in sentiment to much love poetry written by men at the time.

ACTIVITY 55

Debate the idea that the principal concerns of men and women may be different. Apply your ideas to the subjects that women might write about. You could touch on other issues such as the fact that women's roles have changed more than those of men over the years.

Marital bliss

In Shakespeare's comedies marriage is seen as the perfect ending. All the characters are allocated an appropriate spouse – even the novice nun Isabella in *Measure for Measure* appears to marry the Duke.

The Elizabethans, then, saw women often as distant and perfect objects. However, in the tragedies of Shakespeare the dominant women are often more wicked than their husbands. It would be difficult to find women more wicked than Goneril and Regan in *King Lear* and more devious than Cleopatra in *Antony and Cleopatra* and Lady Macbeth. At the same time we have the self-sacrifice of Cordelia in *King Lear* and Juliet in *Romeo and Juliet.*

Restoration Comedy was often based around searching and finding the ideal marriage partner, with the consequent intrigues and deception.

In the late eighteenth and early nineteenth century Jane Austen's novels are mostly centred around finding a perfect and rich partner. One of the most famous opening sentences in literature is that on the subject of marriage at the beginning of *Pride and Prejudice:*

It is a truth universally acknowledged that a single man in possession of a good fortune must be in want of a wife.

In the first half of the nineteenth century we have the two murderers in *My Last Duchess* and *Porphyria's Lover* by Robert Browning. For the narrators of these two poems marriage is not enough and only total possession of the woman will do even if that means in death.

Total possession by a spouse features in a great deal of literature. *Wuthering Heights* by Emily Brontë demonstrates this but here it is the woman whose love is as strong and almost as destructive as the man's. This extract from *Wuthering Heights* demonstrates the all-pervading power of the love Catherine has for Heathcliff. Catherine is considering marrying Edgar Linton so that she can protect and support Heathcliff:

I cannot express it; but surely you and everybody has a notion that there is or should be an existence of yours beyond you. What were the use of my creation, if it were entirely contained here? My great miseries in the world have been Heathcliff's miseries, and I watched and felt each from the beginning: my great thought in living is himself. If all else perished and *he* remained, I should continue to be; and if all else remained and he annihilated, the universe would turn to a mighty stranger: I should not seem part of it. My love for Linton is like the foliage in the woods: time will change it, I'm well aware, as winter changes the trees. My love for Heathcliff resembles the eternal rocks beneath: a source of little visible delight but necessary. Nelly, I *am* Heathcliff!

Here we see a complete reversal of the sentiments of women. Cathy is expressing women's love equally as strongly as any found in the sonnets of the Elizabethan era. Women's emotions are being acknowledged at last. The love of Miriam for Paul in *Sons and Lovers* (1913) and Tess for Angel Clare in *Tess of the d'Urbervilles* (1895) are equally all consuming.

ACTIVITY 56

Charles Dickens' novels are full of examples of different types of marriages. Here is an extract from *Great Expectations* where Joe Gargery explains why he allows Mrs Joe, Pip's sister, to continue to be the dominant and often brutal partner. Joe is a simple but admirable and honest character in the book. What does this passage tell us of the position of some women in Victorian times and Dickens' attitude to this?

I don't deny that your sister comes the Mo-gul over us, now and again. I don't deny that she do throw us back-falls, and that she do drop down on us heavy. At such times as when your sister is on the Ram-page, Pip,' Joe sank his voice to a whisper and glanced at the door, 'candour compels fur to admit that she is a Buster.'
Joe pronounced this word, as if it began with at least twelve capital Bs.
'Why don't I rise? That were your observation when I broke it off, Pip?'
'Yes, Joe'.
'Well,' said Joe, passing the poker into his left hand, that he might feel his whisker; and I had no hope of him whenever he took to that placid occupation; 'your sister's a master-mind. A master-mind.'

'What's that?' I asked, in some hope of bringing him to a stand. But Joe was readier with his definition than I had expected, and completely stopped me arguing circularly, and answering with a fixed look, 'Her'.

'And I ain't a master-mind,' Joe resumed, when he had unfixed his look, and got back to his whisker. 'And last of all Pip – this I want to say very serious to you, old chap – I see so much in my poor old mother, of a woman drudging and slaving and breaking her honest heart and never getting no peace in her mortal days, that I'm dead afeerd of going wrong in the way of not doing what's right by a woman, and I'd fur rather of the two go wrong the t'other way, and be a little inconvenienced myself'.

In the same delightful novel you will find description of the marital bliss of the Pocket family (Chapter 23) and the amusing relationship of Wemmick and Miss Skiffins (Chapter 37) and their wedding (Chapter 55). Pip's eventual marriage to Estella in this novel will be a successful marriage of equals.

Another aspect of marriage in Dickens' books is a consideration of being ready and sensible enough to marry. David Copperfield's wife, Dora, is too beautiful and childish to make a good wife. She accepts her early death as appropriate for an inappropriate wife. This is what she says just before she dies:

Oh, Doady, after more years, you never could have loved your child-wife better than you do; and, after more years, she would so have tried and disappointed you, that you might not have been able to love her half so well! I know I was young and foolish. It is much better as it is!'

After a while David marries the faithful and sensible Agnes whom he has really been devoted to all his life.

Cultural responses to marriage have changed during the final years of the twentieth century and into the twenty-first. More recently we have a more realistic and possibly more cynical attitude to marriage. Fewer people are getting married and partners are as acceptable as spouses in most social circles. In Chapter 3 two poems on the possible positions of women in marriage are reprinted. They are *The Wife's Tale* by Seamus Heaney and *Portrait of a Marriage* by Dannie Abse. You have already had the opportunity of studying these.

ACTIVITY 57

Remind yourself again of *Portrait of a Marriage* in Chapter 3 and then read the poem *Marriage* by Elaine Feinstein printed below. They both express the same sentiments about women and their role in marriage. Women's expectations from a relationship have changed dramatically in the last half century. Make a list of the similarities in the sentiments of the poems.

Marriage

Is there ever a new beginning when every
word has its ten years' weight, can there be
what you call conversation between us?
Relentless you are as you push me
to dance and I lurch away from you
weeping, and yet can we bear to lie

silent under the ice together like
fish in a long winter?

A letter now from York is a reminder of
windless Rievaulx, the hillside moving through
limestone arches, in the ear's liquid the
whir of dove notes: we were a fellowship of three
strangers walking in northern brightness, our
searches peaceful, in the silence the
resonance of stones only, any celebate
could look for such retreat, for me
it was a luxury to be insisted on
in the sight of these grass-overgrown dormitories

We have taken our shape from the
damage we do one another, gently as
bodies moving together at night, we amend
our gestures, softly we hold our places:
in the alien school morning in the
small stones of your eyes I know how
you want to be rid of us, you were
never a family man, your virtue is
lost, even alikeness deceived us
love, our spirits sprawl together
and both at last are distorted

and yet we go toward birthdays and other
marks   not wryly   not thriftily
waiting, for where shall we find it, a
joyous, a various world? in fury
we share, which keeps us, without
resignation: tender whenever we touch   what
else we share   this flesh   we
bring together   it hurts to
think of dying as we lie close.

Elaine Feinstein

COMMENTARY Elaine Feinstein has said that she wants poems that are genuinely trying to make sense of experience. In this poem she is expressing an experience that is probably shared by women all over the world. The first stanza is negative in its attitude. Ten years together has led to each word having overtones which are remembered. 'Relentless', 'push', 'lurch', 'weep' all add to the uneasy atmosphere. The cold and unemotional image of fish under a frozen pond demonstrates their feeling or lack of it. A visit to Rievaulx Abbey merely increased their distance and they were strangers. There is an acceptance of the damage they have done each other and the distortion it has caused in the third stanza. Finally they share only fury and a fear of dying.

The Bloodaxe Book of Contemporary Women Poets edited by Jeni Couzyn (published by Bloodaxe) is a good source of women's writing and has a short commentary by each of the contributors.

Recent roles

In recent years women's roles and position have become more varied. From being simply possessions they have now become more emancipated and expect to be seen as people. This has led to literature where women's dissatisfaction with their position is expressed. This is obvious in the poems we have looked at about marriage. However, this expression of dissatisfaction is not restricted to poetry. Alan Bennett's *Talking Heads* (first series) shows women being both exploited and showing their dissatisfaction. In *Bed Among the Lentils* Susan, the speaker in the monologue, is the wife of a vicar. This is how she sums up her position:

Once upon a time I had my life planned out ... or half of it at any rate. I wasn't clear about the first part, but at the stroke of fifty I was all set to turn into a wonderful woman ... the wife to a doctor, or a vicar's wife, Chairman of the Parish Council, a pillar of the W.I. A wise, witty and ultimately white-haired old lady, who's always stood on her own feet until one day at the age of eighty she comes out of the County Library, falls under the weight of her improving book, breaks her hip and dies peacefully, continently and without fuss under a snowy coverlet in the cottage hospital. And coming away from her funeral in a country churchyard on a bright winter's afternoon people would say, 'well, she was a wonderful woman'.

Had this been a serious ambition I should have seen to it I was equipped with the skills necessary to its achievement. How to produce jam which, after reaching a good, rolling boil, successfully coats the spoon; how to whip up a Victoria sponge that just gives to the finger tips; how to plan, execute and carry through a successful garden fete. All the weapons in the armoury of any upstanding Anglican lady. But I can do none of these things. I'm even a fool at the flower arrangement. I ought to have a PhD in the subject the number of classes I've been to but still my efforts show as much evidence of art as walking sticks in an umbrella stand. Actually it's temperament. I don't have it. If you think squash is a competitive activity try flower arrangement.

In the story Susan, a vicar's wife and an alcoholic, has a torrid affair with the owner of the local off-licence and general store Mr Ramesh. That's rebellion for you! She is, however, brought back to the fold and she is accepted again by the community as a black sheep who has repented. The story is a tragi-comedy which shows how one woman tried to rebel but didn't make it. Alan Bennett, like all accomplished writers, portrays the thoughts and feelings of the opposite sex in a confident and convincing way.

By women – about women

Women writers are now as prevalent as men and as successful. Obviously they write about issues that affect both sexes but often they place more emphasis on female issues and perspectives. *The Penguin Book of Modern Women's Short Stories* edited by Susan Hill makes interesting reading. Here is the blurb from the back cover:

Marriage, motherhood, the battle for self-realisation, bereavement, the louring of old age – women's particular preoccupations thread in and out of our literary history. Susan Hill's collection of short stories by British women reveals the consolidations made during the post-war period as women became more confident about articulating their desires and intimate thoughts. Taken together, the stories drive a tap root into different aspects of the feminine psyche; A.S. Byatt's agonising cry for a dead child in the *July Ghost*; the encounter with self knowledge seen in Patricia Ferguson's nurse on night duty; the tyranny exerted by food which many women will recognise in Angela Huth's *The Weighing Up*; Fay Weldon's sparkling, blackly funny view of a middle-class marriage.

Including contributions by, among others, Penelope Lively, Edna O'Brien, Sara Maitland, Margaret Drabble, Georgina Hammick, Rose Tremain and Elizabeth Jane Howard, this stimulating, entertaining and many layered collection shows women writing easily, confidently and superbly well.

Susan Hill herself comments in the introduction:

These stories are about anger and bitterness, love and loss, loneliness, growing, waste, change, oppression, nostalgia, grief endurance, war, fear, death. They move one to tears, to laughter, to pity, to despair, and to admiration at fine writing. But perhaps most importantly, they move the reader to give a cry of recognition and understanding – yes, this is what it feels like to be human in this way – time and time again. It goes without saying that they may equally well be read and enjoyed by both sexes, but perhaps they do speak, at a certain level, very particularly to women.

Weekend by Fay Weldon is the final story in the collection. It is a black comedy about a middle-class family and their 'relaxing' weekend at their weekend cottage where they also entertain visitors. Here is one paragraph to give you a flavour of the role of the mother in this family.

On Fridays Martha would get home on the bus at six-twelve and prepare tea and sandwiches for the family; then she would strip the beds and put the sheets and quilt covers in the washing machine for Monday; take the country bedding from the airing basket, plus the books and games, plus the weekend food acquired at intervals throughout the week, to lessen the load – plus her own folder of work from the office, plus Martin's drawing materials (she was a market researcher in an advertising agency, he a freelance designer) plus hairbrushes, jeans, spare T-shirts, Jolyon's antibiotics (he suffered from sore throats), Jenny's recorder, Jasper's cassette player and so on – ah, the so on! – and would pack them all, skilfully and quickly, into the boot. Very little could be left in the cottage during the week. ('An open invitation to burglars'; Martin). Then Martha would run round the house tidying and wiping, doing this and that, finding the cat at the neighbour's and delivering it to another, while the others ate their tea; and would usually, proudly, have everything finished by the time they had eaten their fill. Martin would just catch the BBC2 news, while Martha cleared away the tea table, and the children tossed up for the best positions in the car. 'Martha,' said Martin, tonight, 'you ought to get Mrs Hodder to do more. She takes advantage of you.'

Fay Weldon is here showing us how the present position of women is gradually eroding once more so that women are expected to be and do everything brilliantly and they agree to this proposition and often take a pride in being superwoman. What is the price of women's equality in this situation?

The position of women has changed and is still changing. In this section we have suggested this by looking historically at attitudes to women and marriage by both men and women in literature of various types and from various periods. We have looked at a variety of forms of literature to establish trends where we could. In this section we have linked texts by looking at a particular aspect of the culture of a society in loosely historical terms, i.e. the position of women.

Black women

Now let's look at the poetry of two black women writers. Black women poets are usually lively and engaging. Two such writers are Grace Nichols and Maya Angelou.

Grace Nichols was born in Guyana in 1950. She worked as a journalist and came to Britain in 1977 and published a collection of poetry called *The Fat Black Woman's Poems* in the early eighties.

Maya Angelou was born in 1928 and was raised in the southern states of America. As well as being a critic and prose writer Angelou also has written a great deal of poetry.

Both women feature political and social commentary in their poems and also have a sense of humour in their approach to their position and appearance. These women show defiance and resilience in the face of racial and sexual discrimination. The tone of much of their work is similiar. What issues are likely to be addressed in poetry written by black women in the middle of the twentieth century?

Texts can be linked by the cultural background of the writers. Black women have particular experiences and their work can be linked by their writing about these experiences and their reactions to them.

Maya Angelou's autobiography *I Know Why the Caged Bird Sings* and the fictional letters of Alice Walker in *The Color Purple* are a good source of comparison – black women writing about the experiences of black women at approximately the same time and in the same social climate. Angelou's autobiography is episodic in structure with vivid accounts of a few specific incidents which undoubtedly have a basis in reality. These must be considered as representative of many other similar encounters. Walker's book, however, is in the form of an epistolary novel with a fictional narrator. (There is obviously scope here for comparing other epistolary novels.) The effect of these two different structures on the style and content is well worth investigating.

In both of these texts similar incidents of abuse are described. Maya Angelou in her autobiography describes when her mother's lover raped her and in *The Color Purple* Alice Walker describes her fictional narrator Celie being raped by the man she calls father. These two texts are set in the same cultural background – in a culture where black people were still fighting against the remnants of slavery and where, within their own culture, women were treated as objects.

Find a copy of *The Color Purple* by Alice Walker and *I Know Why the Caged Bird Sings* by Maya Angelou. Study the first two letters in *The Color Purple* and the first nine paragraphs of Chapter 12 of *I Know Why the Caged Bird Sings*. What are the similarities and differences in the ways the incidents are described? Try to be as specific as you can about the language each writer uses. Look at the use of speech and its effect. Look also at the childish euphemisms for sexual parts. Notice that the letters are contemporary to the event and the second text is written in later years with some reflective aspects and discuss the effect of this.

Investigate the poetry of Grace Nichols and Maya Angelou. Three suitable poems by each are:

Grace Nichols
– Fat Black Woman Remembers
– Fat Black Woman Goes Shopping
– Fat Black Woman Versus Politics

Maya Angelou
– Preacher, Don't Send Me
– Riot 60's
– Phenomenal Woman

Other Big Issues

Attitudes to children, and childhood, attitudes to nature or the destruction of it, attitudes to technology, attitudes to rural and urban surroundings – these will prove quite useful areas to pursue in your search for suitable cultural connections.

Stop press

What are the most pressing issues of today? Homelessness, pollution, medical advances, global warming, political issues, corruption in high places, the technological revolution, the role of work and the rights of women and minority groups ... Look out for modern poems on these themes and see how they are portrayed. You may find it fairly difficult to find poems on these issues but quality magazines and newspapers are probable sources. Literature is still basically about love, death, loss, war and the basic human vices of greed and jealousy. Although the themes may recur, the language in which they are expressed will vary as will the attitudes.

Whistle while you work!

And finally here are two poems on the subject of work – something common to all cultures. Identify the cultural issues at work in them.

You may need to look up something about the cultural background of each poet. Go on to identify similarities and differences in form and style.

Toads

Why should I let the toad work
Squat on my life?
Can't I use my wit as a pitchfork
And drive the brute off?

Six days of the week it soils
With its sickening poison –
Just for paying a few bills!
That's out of proportion.

Lots of folks live on their wits:
Lecturers, lispers,
Losels, loblolly-men, louts
They don't end as paupers;

Lots of folks live up lanes
With fires in a bucket,
Eat windfalls and tinned sardines –
They seem to like it.

Their nippers have got bare feet,
Their unspeakable wives
Are skinny as whippets – and yet
No one actually starves.

Ah, were I courageous enough
To shout *Stuff your pension!*
But I know, all too well, that's the stuff
That dreams are made on:

For something sufficiently toad-like
squats in me, too;
Its hunkers are heavy as hard luck,
And cold as snow,

And will never allow me to blarney
My way to getting
The fame and the girl and the money
All at one sitting.

I don't say, one bodies the other
One's spiritual truth;
But I do say it's hard to lose either
When you have both.

Philip Larkin

The Solitary Reaper

Behold her, single in the field,
Yon solitary Highland Lass!
Reaping and singing by herself;

Stop here or gently pass!
Alone she cuts and binds the grain,
And sings a melancholy strain;
O listen! for the vale profound
Is overflowing with the sound.

No nightingale did ever chaunt
More welcome notes to weary bands
Of travellers in some shady haunt,
Among Arabian sands;
A voice so thrilling ne'er was heard
In spring-time from the cuckoo-bird,
Breaking the silence of the seas
Among the farthest Hebrides.

Will no-one tell me what she sings?
Perhaps the plaintive numbers flow
For old unhappy, far-off things,
And battles long ago:
Or is it some more humble lay,
Familiar matter of today?
Some natural sorrow, loss or pain,
That has been, and may be again?

Whate'er the theme, the maiden sang
As if her song could have no ending;
I saw her singing at her work,
And o'er her sickle bending;
I listen'd, motionless and still;
And, as I mounted up the hill,
The music in my heart I bore,
Long after it was heard no more.

William Wordsworth

So, then, the cultural context of texts is worth exploring. Movements and trends can be identified. Political and social issues are tackled, particularly in prose. Contemporary issues can be recognised. We've looked at war, women and finally glanced at work.

Answers to Activity 50:

1914–18	Text B *The Letter* (Wilfred Owen)
1939–45	Text D *Air Raid* (Charles Robinson)
Vietnam	Text C *What Were They Like?* (Denise Levertov)
Nuclear War	Text E *Your Attention Please* (Peter Porter)
Falklands	Text A *My Family* (Paul D. Wapshott)
Ireland	Text F *The Identification* (Roger McGough)

5 Language and Structure – the Basics

In this final chapter we are going to look in detail at stylistics and also at the effect that structure and narrative technique have on the style of a piece of writing. You probably have a good working knowledge of style already as you are well into your English course.

Spot the difference

As a child you probably 'had a go' at competitions in comics or magazines. There would be two pictures and you had to spot a large number of minute differences – for example the number of spots on the curtains or the Dalmatian dog or the number of stripes on the wallpaper. You may have found this rewarding – although you may have found it frustrating too. Comparing detailed differences between two pictures is like comparing and linking two very similar texts from the point of view of style. It is the stylistic analysis which is the subtle and sometimes difficult aspect of literary comparison. We are putting the texts under a microscope and we have to be able to describe and understand what we see.

Intuition

When you read a text you may pick up the nuances of meaning intuitively. You 'get a feeling' for what the writer is saying. It is likely that other readers get the same or very similar feelings. What you need to be able to do is identify *why* you get these feelings and how they are provoked in you by the writer. You need to ask yourself 'How do I know that?' The question 'how?' is more difficult than the question 'what?'

As you are reading this textbook, you are probably a second year English student who has already accumulated a great deal of the stylistic knowledge you need to link texts. It may be latent but it will be there! In this chapter we shall consolidate your knowledge and fill in any gaps.

Asking questions

You will be asking yourself who, what, why, how, and when, with most emphasis on the 'how'. It is the 'how' that leads on to a study of the style of a text.

What does it mean?

A person can have 'style'. You would be pleased and flattered if the word were applied to you as it means having a certain flair, looking good, behaving well, knowing what to do when, never being awkward or out of place, admired by all! The word has a different meaning when used about literature. In this sense it has to do with the way something is written – the 'how?' It refers to the form, the word choice, the sentence length, the use of imagery. Your job is to identify the features of style and then comment on their effectiveness or appropriateness. You need a basic tool kit to do this.

Other resources

There are sections on stylistics in other books in this series.

You might like to consult these, all published by Hodder and Stoughton:

Living Language: Language and Style by Michael Jago in the *Living Language* series

Living Literature, Chapter 6, 'How language shapes texts' by Frank Myszor and Jackie Baker

Living Language and Literature, Chapter 4, 'Language Roundabout' by George Keith and John Shuttleworth

Living Language, Chapter 6, 'Grammar in action', and Chapter 9, 'Stylistics' by George Keith and John Shuttleworth

Living Language: Language and Literature, Chapter 2, 'Literary Stylistics' by George Keith in the *Living Language* series.

The really useful list

This is really the basic terminology, the basic tool kit, that you cannot do without. It would be surprising if you'd got this far without encountering most of these! You are in fact required to use appropriate terminology (Assessment Objective 1) and show how writers' choices of language 'shape meanings' (Assessment Objective 3) in your A level work. The top band on the examiners' marking grids requires students to be credited for 'extensive appropriate critical vocabulary'.

Grammar matters

This list is based on a simple 'need to know' principle.

Nouns

- abstract
- concrete
- proper

Adjectives

- also called modifiers, tell you more about the noun.
- can be comparative, i.e. the *fastest* car or the *slower* reader

Verbs

- tense
- active/passive
- imperative

Adverbs

- tell you more about the verb
- answer the question 'how?'

Sentence types

- simple – one main idea, one main verb
- compound – two or more main ideas and verbs connected by words like 'and', 'but' or 'or'. Both parts of the sentence seem to have equal 'worth'
- complex – two or more main ideas which seem to depend on or relate to each other in some way. Connecting words – 'if', 'unless', 'while', 'when', 'as'.
- purpose – statements/commands/questions/exclamations

Other matters

Other features to remember are:

Lexical features – the types of words used (this will depend on the purpose and audience)

- formal/informal

- technical/non-technical
- standard/non-standard

Semantic features – the area of meaning and use of words

- semantic field
- figurative language/imagery (metaphors and similes)

Phonological features (to do with sound)

- assonance
- alliteration
- rhythm
- rhyme
- patterning
- repetition

Poetry matters

All the features above can be applied to poetry but the features listed here refer specifically to poetry.

- form (sonnet, ballad, free verse, ode, etc.)
- rhyme (couplet, quatrain, half rhyme, eye rhyme)
- rhythm (the regular stressed words in a poem, the patterning caused by this)
- figurative language (the use of metaphor, simile)

Putting this into practice

Let's take a detailed look at some of the texts we have already considered as possible comparisons. Remember that you are trying to identify features of the texts and then comment on the significance of these features. What you find may be unexpected.

Two schools of thought

In Chapter 1 we looked at two extracts describing two different school situations. First of all we'll consider Charles Dickens' portrayal of a school in *Hard Times*.

ACTIVITY 61

Read the extract from *Hard Times* in Chapter 1 again (p. 17) and consider the nouns, verbs, modifiers, patterning and figurative language.

COMMENTARY It is not difficult to count the number of times the noun 'facts' appears and this makes the subject matter quite clear to the reader! The schoolroom is a 'vault' which implies being locked up without air to breathe in a cold unfriendly environment. The speaker's forehead is a 'wall' which suggests his mind is solid and impenetrable. There is no compromise in this man as all his features are described with the modifier 'square'. The boys and girls are unadorned by modifiers. They are bare and empty. The schoolroom itself has three modifiers, 'plain', 'bare', 'monotonous'. The speaker's voice also has three modifiers, all rather threatening – 'inflexible', 'dry' and 'dictatorial'. The use of the verb 'emphasised' followed by the noun 'emphasis' again shows the lack of tolerance and sympathy. The repeated structure 'the emphasis was …' again reiterates the inflexible message. There is also a feeling of formality in the language with words such as 'commodious cellerage' and 'unaccommodating grasp'.

The spoken words at the beginning of the extract are abrupt with short simple or compound sentences. No room for compromise here! The verbs are in the imperative form 'teach', 'plant', 'root', 'stick'.

The figurative language adds a touch of humour with the personification of the neckcloth as relentless in its grasp at the speaker's throat and the simile describing the bumps on the speaker's head as 'like the crust of a plum pie' – no doubt the young pupils would enjoy the comparison.

The final metaphor is apt and convincing. The pupils were simply waiting like 'empty vessels' to be filled with facts.

ACTIVITY 62

Now look at the extract from *Cider with Rosie* in Chapter 1 (p. 16). The book is autobiographical and therefore written in the first person.

Study this extract in the light of its use of nouns, verbs, modifiers, patterning and figurative language.

COMMENTARY You will soon see that the emphasis in the extract is different from that in the extract from *Hard Times*. A lot of information about the pupils is given by the use of modifiers. They are certainly not 'empty vessels'. They are described as 'wild' and bringing with them 'strange oaths and odours, quaint garments and curious pies'. They are collectively called the 'rabble'. Their clothes are clearly described with modifiers 'old, ragged and torn'. The girls have 'frizzled hair' and the boys are 'huge' with 'sharp elbows'. All are effectively described with the interesting observation of a child.

The direct speech is dialectal and realistically portrays the children's speech, for example 'I ain't, I'm stoppin' 'ome'. The text as a whole has a sense of informality with expressions like the school was 'one up' on that of the grandparents and he 'swiped' somebody's apple.

The verbs are not imperative but frequently suggest the feelings of the narrator, 'I didn't expect', 'I felt', 'I was rescued' and 'I swiped'. This shows that in this environment thoughts and feelings count!

There is some patterning in the balance of 'universal education' and 'unusual fertility', 'skating' and 'skidding'.

There are several simple similes – 'the playground roared like a rodeo', 'grit flew in my face like shrapnel', the counting frame the teacher played 'like a harp', he was spun round 'like a top'. All these are vivid and simple images. The variety of imagery shows the independence of the children as opposed to the restriction of the 'vault' with its 'empty vessels' in the extract from *Hard Times*.

Although there is a variety of sentence length, the sentences tend to be simple or compound and often read with the simplicity of a list.

So *Hard Times* begins with its stern restrictive schoolroom which is intended to stifle individuality. The modifiers demonstrate the emphasis on fact and the inability to deviate from squareness! *Cider with Rosie* shows a school full of individuals who will be allowed to flourish. They are described with a wide variety of modifiers showing the individuality of the pupils.

Fact and fiction

Let's look now at two texts on almost exactly the same topic using the same source material and published at roughly the same time. Both rely on contemporary reports, diaries, letters and journals for their sources.

The Fatal Shore by Robert Hughes has the subtitle *A History of the Transportation of Convicts to Australia 1787–1868*.

The blurb on the cover describes the book as:

An epic description of the brutal transportation of men, women and children out of Georgian Britain into a horrific penal system which was to be the precursor to the Gulag and was the origin of Australia. *The Fatal Shore* is the prize-winning, scholarly, brilliantly entertaining narrative that has given its true history to Australia.

The Playmaker by Thomas Keneally is about the production of a Restoration Comedy by the first convicts to be deported to Australia.

The blurb on the cover says:

In 1789 in Sydney Cove, the remotest penal colony of the British Empire, a group of convicts and one of their captors unite to stage a play. As felons, perjurers and whores rehearse, their playmaker becomes seduced. For the play's power is mirrored in the rich, varied life of this primitive land and, not least in the convict actress, Mary Brenham.

ACTIVITY 63

One of these books is a history; the other is a novel based on some true facts.

Discuss what features you would expect to find in each book. What do you think the major differences would be, given the different purposes?

If you came up with ideas about the depth of characterisation and the level of factual information you are on the right lines. As we look at some extracts from the texts you may find some surprises!

Sydney over 200 years before the 2000 Olympics

ACTIVITY 64

Below is an extract from Chapter 1 of *The Fatal Shore*.

Study the style of it carefully looking for the stylistic features you have been reminded of in this chapter. Remember this is a history book and decide if this was what you were expecting!

One may liken this moment to the breaking open of a capsule. Upon the harbour ships were now entering. European history had left no mark at all. Until the swollen sails and curvetting bows of the British fleet came round South Head, there were no dates. The Aborigines and the fauna around them had possessed the landscape since time immemorial, and no other human eye had seen them. Now the protective glass of distance broke, in an instant, never to be restored.

To imagine the place, one should begin at North Head, the upper mandible of the harbour. Here Australia stops; its plates of sandstone break off like a biscuit whose crumbs, the size of cottages, lie jumbled 250 feet below, at the surging ultramarine rim of the Pacific. A ragged wall of creamy-brown sandstone, fretted by the incessant wind, runs north to a glazed horizon. To the east, the pacific begins its 7,000 mile arc toward South America. Long swells grind into the cliff in a boiling white lather, flinging veils of water a hundred feet into the air. At the meeting of its ancient planes of rock, sea and sky – mass, energy and light – one can grasp why the Aborigines called North Head *Boree*, 'the enduring one'.

The sandstone is the bone and root of the coast. On top of the cliff, the soil is thin and the scrub sparse. There are banksia bushes, with their sawtooth-edge leaves and dried seed-cones like multiple, jabbering mouths. Against this austere gray-green, the occasional red or blue scribble of a flower looks startling. But further back to the west, the sandstone ledges dip down to the harbour, separating into scores of inlets. In 1788 these sheltered coves were densely wooded. The largest trees were eucalypts: red gums, angophoras, scribbly gums and a dozen others. Until the late eighteenth century no European had ever seen a eucalypt, and very strange they must have looked, with their strings of hanging, half shed bark, their smooth wrinkling joints (like armpits, elbows or crotches), their fluent gesticulations and haze of perennial foliage. Not evergreens but evergrays: the soft spatially deceitful background color of the Australian bush, monotonous-looking at first sight but rippling with nuance to the acclimatised eye.

In the gullies, where streams of water slid from pool to pool leaving beards of rusty algae on their sand stone lips, giant cabbage tree palms grew, their damp shade supporting a host of ferns and mosses. Yellow sprays of mimosa flashed in the sun along the ridges, and there were strands of blackboy trees, their dry spear of a stalk shooting up from a drooping hackle of fronds.

Most of the ground was sandy and thin, but parts of the harbour foreshores held, to the relief of Captain John Hunter, Phillip's second in command,

Tolerable land ... which may be cultivated without waiting for its being cleared of wood, for the trees stand very wide of one another, and have no underwood, in short, the woods ... resemble a deer park, as much as if they had been intended for the purpose.

You have probably noticed the use of figurative language (metaphors and similes). You may have also noticed some personification. The nouns in the extract are heavily modified to depict colour, sight, and texture. The sentence length varies. The factual information is almost hidden in the rather poetic prose we have here!

The final part of the extract shows how Hughes weaves in his source material by quoting short sections and stating the writer.

This extract shows a surprising literary merit for what might be called a factual text.

An extract from *The Playmaker* follows. The same place is being described. How is it different from the previous extract?

> The place which had been chosen for this far-off commonwealth and prison, and named Sydney Cove in the spirit of events, faced the sun, which was always in the north. This reminded you, if you thought about it, that home was always on the other side of the sun – eight moons of navigation away if you were lucky, a year or more if you were not. The land on either side of the cove was divided down the middle by a freshwater stream flowing out of the hinterland among the cabbage-tree palms, native cedars, the strange, obdurate eucalyptus trees of a type which (as Ralph was assured by scholars like Davy), occurred nowhere else in all Creation. Ralph had not liked to say, in the face of Davy's botanical excitement, that the rest of the world had been lucky to miss out on these twisted, eccentric plants. But if, as Dick Johnson believed, it was the great flood of Noah which had drowned the unlovely eucalypts elsewhere than here, then elsewhere than here were lucky to have missed them.
>
> There was a steely tree too which when struck with the axe either took a gap out of the blade or began to bleed a blood-red sap. It was, Ralph thought, a fair symbol not only of the strangeness of this reach of space but of the criminal soul as well.

You will have noticed that the description is less evocative and less poetic! The eucalyptus trees are for Ralph modified by the words 'obdurate', 'unlovely', 'twisted', 'eccentric'.

The metaphorical language takes the form of a threatening symbol of the bleeding tree in which Ralph sees a symbol for the convicts. This text is written in the third person but it is mostly from the viewpoint of one of the main characters, the producer of the play, Ralph Clark.

In the novel *The Playmaker* the characters come alive for us. We follow their hopes, fears, love affairs, lies, triumphs, defeats. We also hear about their digestive problems, drinking problems and their toothache!

In *The Fatal Shore* Hughes is not always as poetic as he was in the first extract.

Read this extract to see the difference:

> Who were these First Fleet convicts? It was once a cherished Australian belief that at least some of the people on the First Fleet were political exiles – rick-burners, trade unionists, and the like. In fact, though victims of a savage penal code, they were not political prisoners. On the other hand, few of them were dangerous criminals. Not one person was shipped out in 1787 for murder or rape, although more than a hundred of them had been convicted of thefts (such as highway robbery) in which violence played some part. No woman in the first fleet, legend to the contrary, had been transported for prostitution, as it was not a transportable offence. Many were treated

as whores, and doubtless some were, although only two – Mary Allen and Ann Mather – had been described by their judges as 'unfortunate girl' or 'poor unhappy woman of the town'.

This section in the original text is followed by a commentary on three charts which show a breakdown of the crimes of the convicts, their ages, and finally their trade.

The passage above has some characteristics of factual/historical writing in that some of the sentences are complex. The conjunctions 'although' and 'as' connect subordinate clauses thus showing the writer is arguing his point and giving evidence. Notice how Hughes seems to be rather superior to his fellow Australians. He uses the modifier 'cherished' as he implies that they were deluding themselves as he proves that none of the first convict settlers were of the political category – rather they were simply petty thieves who had been unfortunate enough to be caught. The tone is one of superiority.

The connectives 'in fact' and 'on the other hand' are also typical of informative writing.

To complete the picture, let's look at Bill Bryson's bestseller *Down Under*. This is about his travels in Australia but early in the book he tackles the issue of the convict settlers.

Of the roughly one thousand people who shuffled ashore, about 700 were prisoners and the rest were marines and officers, officers' families and the governor and his staff. The exact numbers of each are not known, but it hardly matters. They were all prisoners now.

   They were, to put it mildly, a curious lot. The complement included a boy of nine and a woman of eighty-two – hardly the sort of people you would invite to help you through an ordeal. Though it had been noted in London that certain skills would be desirable in such a remote location, no one had actually acted on that observation. The party included no-one proficient in natural sciences, no master of husbandry, not a soul who had the faintest understanding of growing crops in hostile climes. The prisoners were in nearly every practical respect woeful. Among the 700 there was just one fisherman and no more than five people with a working knowledge of the building trade. Phillip was by all accounts a kindly man of even temper and natural honesty, but his situation was hopeless. Confronted with a land full of plants he had never seen and knew nothing about, he recorded in despair; 'I am without a botanist, or even an intelligent gardener'.

Bryson has his usual light touch here. Notice the alliteration in 'shuffles ashore' which makes you see their drudgery clearly but also sounds quite comical. Notice also his use of archaic words (words which are old-fashioned or out of date), for example 'woeful', 'hostile climes', 'complement' and 'husbandry'. Notice the change in the level of formality with the use of the more colloquial expression 'curious lot'. The equivalent expression in Hughes' book is 'motley crew' which is perhaps more formal and even archaic.

ACTIVITY 65

Now it's your turn

As you can see comparisons of style need close study. It would not really be possible or interesting to base a whole piece of work of any length on style alone. However, when you can comment on detailed stylistic features it is impressive!

Here are two descriptions of beaches. See what stylistic similarities and differences you can find.

Extract from *The Beach* by Alex Garland:

At first glance the camp was close to how I'd imagined it might be. There was a large dusty clearing surrounded by the rocket-ship trees and dotted with makeshift bamboo huts. A few canvas tents looked incongruous, but otherwise it was very like the South-East-Asian village I'd seen many times before. At the far end was a larger construction, a long house, and beside it the stream from the waterfall re-emerged, bending around to run along the edge of the clearing. From the straightness of its banks, it had obviously been deliberately diverted.

It was only after taking all this in that I noticed there was something strange about the light. The forest had been both dark and bright by turns, but here everything was light in an unchanging twilight, more like dusk than midday. I looked up, following the trunk of one of the giant trees. The height of the tree alone was breathtaking, accentuated by the fact that the lower branches had been cut away, so it was possible to appreciate its size. Higher up the branches began to grow again, curving upwards across the clearing like gables until they joined with the branches from the other side. But their point of joining seemed too dense and thick, and as I looked harder I began to see that they were coiled around each other, intertwining to form a cavernous ceiling of wood and leaves, hanging with the stalactite vines that now became magically appropriate.

Extract from *Lord of the Flies* by William Golding:

Here the beach was interrupted abruptly by the square motif of the landscape; a great platform of pink granite thrust up uncompromisingly through the forest and terrace and sand and lagoon to make a raised jetty four feet high. The top of this was covered with a thin layer of soil and coarse grass and shaded with young palm trees. There was not enough soil for them to grow to any height and when they reached perhaps twenty feet they fell and dried, forming a criss-cross pattern of trunks, very convenient to sit on. The palms that stood made a green roof, covered on the underside with the quivering tangle of reflections from the lagoon. Ralph hauled himself on to this platform, noted the coolness and shade, shut one eye, and decided the shadows on his body really were green. He picked his way to the seaward edge of the platform and stood looking down into the water. It was clear to the bottom and bright with the efflorescence of tropical weed and coral. A school of tiny green fish flickered hither and thither. Ralph spoke to himself, sounding the bass strings of delight.
'Whizzoh'.

You may have linked these texts for some of these reasons:

- Both pieces describe colour
- The first passage is more figurative
- One is written in the first person and one in the third
- The interference of man is already obvious in the first one.

If you would like to consider another famous story about a deserted island you might like to look at *Robinson Crusoe*. In fact there is very little description of the island in this book but there is a lot of detail about the thoughts and feelings of Robinson Crusoe himself and how he manages to survive.

Seasonal selection

Let's look now at two poems about the season of Autumn.

One of the most famous poems about this season is *Ode to Autumn* by John Keats. Another poem about the activities connected with Autumn which is almost as famous is *Blackberry Picking* by Seamus Heaney.

ACTIVITY 66

Study the poems *Ode To Autumn* by John Keats and *Blackberry Picking* by Seamus Heaney carefully and make a systematic analysis based on these factors.

1 List the appeals to the senses in both (sight, sound, touch, taste and smell)
2 List the lines that rhyme and see if there is a pattern. See what other sound patterns you can find.
3 List the figurative language (metaphors and similes)
4 Make a comment on the variety of sentence length

5 Look at the final lines and see where the poem is leading.

Now look in particular at *Ode To Autumn* and list the verbs which create the personification of Autumn in stanza two. Now find the verbs which create the semantic field of ripeness particularly in stanza one.

Now look in particular at *Blackberry Picking* pick out any expressions which seem to see the events from the point of view of a child. You should find similes, nouns and a coined (made-up) verb.

Ode to Autumn

Season of mists and mellow fruitfulness,
Close bosom friend of the maturing sun;
Conspiring with him how to load and bless
With fruit the vines that round the thatch eaves run,
To bend with apples the mossed cottage-trees,
And fill all fruit with ripeness to the core;
To swell the gourd and plump the hazel shells
With a sweet kernel; to set budding, more,
And still more, later flowers for the bees,
Until they think warm days will never cease,
For Summer has o'er-brimmed their clammy cells.

Who hath not seen thee oft amid thy store?
Sometimes whoever seeks abroad may find
Thee sitting carelessly on a granary floor,
Thy hair soft-lifted by the winnowing wind;
Or on a half-reaped furrow sound asleep,
Drowsed with the fume of poppies, while thy hook

Spares the next swath and all its twined flowers;
And some times like gleaner thou dost keep
Steady thy laden head across a brook;
Or by a cider press, with patient look,
Thou watchest the last oozings hour by hours.

Where are the songs of Spring? Ay, where are they?
Think not of them, thou hast thy music too, –
While barred clouds bloom the soft dying day,
And touch the stubble-plains with rosy hue;
Then in a wailful choir, the small gnats mourn
Among the river sallows, borne aloft
Or sinking as the light wind lives or dies;
And full-grown lambs loud bleat from hilly bourn;
Hedge crickets sing; and now with treble soft
The redbreast whistles from a garden-croft,
And gathering swallows twitter in the skies.

John Keats

Blackberry Picking

Late August, given heavy rain and sun
For a full week, the blackberries would ripen.
At first, just one, a glossy purple clot
Among others, red, green, hard as a knot.
You ate that first one and its flesh was sweet
Like thickened wine: summer's blood was in it
Leaving stains upon the tongue and lust for
Picking. Then red ones inked up and that hunger
Sent us out with milk-cans, pea-tin, jam-pots
Where briars scratched and wet grass bleached our boots.
Round hayfields, cornfields and potato-drills
We trekked and picked until the cans were full,
Until the tinkling bottom had been covered
With green ones, and on the top big dark blobs burned
Like a plate of eyes. Our hands were peppered
With thorn pricks, our palms sticky as Bluebeard's.

We hoarded the fresh berries in the byre.
But when the bath was filled we found a fur,
A rat grey fungus, glutting on our cache.
The juice was stinking too. Once off the bush
The fruit fermented, the sweet flesh would turn sour.
I always felt like crying. It wasn't fair
That all the lovely canfuls smelt of rot.
Each year I hoped they'd keep, knew they would not.

Seamus Heaney

ACTIVITY 67

More Autumn poetry
Now you have got to grips with these two
poems you may like to have a look at a third.

This is another poem about the season of
Autumn. In what ways is it similar to the other
two poems in terms of style?

The Burning of the Leaves

Now is the time for the burning of leaves.
They go to the fire; the nostril pricks with smoke
Wandering slowly into the weeping mist.
Brittle and blotched, ragged and rotten sheaves!
A flame seizes the smouldering ruin, and bites
On stubborn stalks that crackle as they resist.

Now is the time for stripping the spirit bare,
Time for the burning of days ended and done
Idle solace of things that have gone before,
Rootless hope and fruitless desire are there:
Let them go to the fire with never a look behind.
That world that was ours is a world that is ours no more.

They will come again, the leaf and the flower, to arise

From squalor of rottenness into the old splendour,
And magical scents to a wondering memory bring;
The same glory, to shine upon different eyes.
Earth cares for her own ruins, naught for ours.
Nothing is certain, only the certain spring.

                                                              Lawrence Binyon

If you look at this poem carefully you will notice that it is sensuous like the other two. It also uses metaphorical language and personification. It has an established rhyme scheme and some patterning.

You might like to discuss what you think the themes of these three poems are. The poetic techniques are very apparent and similar. Are the themes as easy to decipher?

You should have been trying to use some of the terminology from the 'really useful list'. It is easy to forget to use specific terms but use them if you can.

ACTIVITY 68

By now you have studied these three seasonal poems in some detail. Write a detailed comparison of the three poems showing their links through similarities and differences.

Structural stuff

Texts are often made more interesting because of the structural decisions that the author makes. A story simply told from the beginning to the end may be fine but often a story is more interesting if the reader is anticipating some event that has been predicted or mentioned. In *Silas Marner* by George Eliot there are three essential pieces of information which the reader is told. One is that the child adopted by Marner is the child of the eldest son of the Squire. Another is that the younger son of the Squire stole Marner's money and the third explains that Marner is a recluse because of the unfair treatment he received at the hands of his friends years earlier. This, of course, adds to the intrigue and suspense of the book. The reader anticipates the revelation of these important facts. The revelation of who stole the money leads to the revelation of the father of the child. Marner's strange behaviour throughout is explained by his past. The author has manipulated the information to intrigue the reader.

One of the most complex novels from the point of view of structure is *Wuthering Heights* by Emily Brontë. It is likely that you have read this. It starts with the housekeeper telling a visitor the history of the family she works for. But this is only the middle of the story. The visitor returns years later to hear the final stages of the dramatic tale. *Brideshead Revisited* by Evelyn Waugh has a similar structure with one of the characters in the story remembering events as he returns to a place after years of absence.

Stories are often also more intriguing if they are told from a particular viewpoint. Perhaps from the point of view of some one who comments on the action whether they are part of it or not.

Here we can look briefly at two other aspects of structure – the role of the narrator(s) and the use of flashbacks.

Who is the narrator?

Think of an occasion where you have been told of an event by two different people. You may remember that the emphasis and tone may have been quite different in the two different versions. Perhaps even a different outcome was narrated. The stories you were listening to were told from a different point of view and this is a key factor in novels.

All novels are obviously written by a novelist. However, the actual telling of the story of the novel is more complex than this. A story must be told by someone and this 'someone' has a 'point of view' or a particular stance from which they are telling the story. 'Point of view' should not be confused with 'opinion'. We are not really looking here at what some one thinks about a subject but more about the eyes through which they are telling the story, whether they are an important part of the story or whether they are 'the fly on the wall'. It is important to distinguish between the author and the narrator. Establishing the 'point of view' of a novel is interesting and intriguing.

Here are the main possibilities.

(a) The author tells the story as if he or she knows everything. This is called the omniscient narrator. It is a third person narrative in which the narrator describes the characters as 'he/she' and describes what they do. We are introduced to all the thoughts and feelings of the major characters and the narrator has all the information and chooses when to tell the reader. Sometimes suspense is created here by the reader knowing more than the characters and anticipating what will happen when the character does finally have all the information. Within this category the narrator can be :
   1 objective (telling the story from a balanced and unbiased view point – rather an unlikely aim in literature).
   2 subjective (making judgements and commenting on the action) for example, Jane Austen, George Eliot.
   3 intrusive (pointing out that this is a story or hinting about what will happen next). This could also be called a self-conscious narrator. *Tom Jones* is an example of this. If the narrator has an axe to grind the novel is 'didactic'.
   4 unobtrusive – the reader is unaware of the storyteller. This is the unselfconscious narrator.
(b) The author narrates the story as above but concentrates on telling the story mostly through the eyes of one of the main characters. The reader then has a restricted view of events. This would give a subjective/biased

point of view. It also leads to suspense. Jane Austen's *Emma* is a good example of this.

(c)   The story can be told by one of the characters in the novel – 'a persona'. This means that we have all the thoughts and feelings and also the misconceptions of the character. The story is told in the first person – that is 'I saw' and 'I went' etc. This narrator can of course be reliable or unreliable. Is the character really telling the truth to the reader/himself? Does the character only see what he wants to see or does he misinterpret what happens? Pip misinterprets the actions of Biddy in *Great Expectations*, the eponymous hero of *David Copperfield* by Charles Dickens does not realise that Agnes loves him and that he loves her not as a brother but as a lover. This leads to a great deal of interest for the reader who can agree/disagree or be misled or feel superior! The style can be fairly straightforward narrative or it can echo the confused emotions and thoughts of the narrator. *Brideshead Revisited* is a good example as is *Wuthering Heights*. This latter type of writing taken to its extreme, where the thought processes are expressed, is called 'steam of consciousness'. *As I lay Dying* by William Faulkner is an example of this.

The point of view from which the story is told, then, has a significant effect on the information disclosed to the reader.

Some examples

Here is an extract from *Silas Marner* by George Eliot.

In the days when the spinning wheels hummed busily in the farm houses – and even great ladies, clothed in silk and threadlace, had their toy spinning wheels of polished oak – there might be seen, in districts far away among the lanes, or deep in the bosom of the hills, certain pallid undersized men, who, by the side of the brawny country folk, looked like the remnants of a disinherited race. The shepherd's dog barked fiercely when one of these alien looking men appeared on the upland . . .
   The shepherd himself, though he had reason to believe that the bag held nothing but flaxen thread, or else the long rolls of strong linen spun from that thread, was not quite sure that this trade of weaving, indispensable though it was, could be carried on entirely without the help of the Evil One. In that far off time superstition clung easily round every person or thing that was at all unwonted, or even intermittent and occasional merely, like the visits of the peddler or the knife-grinder. No-one knew where wandering men had their homes or their origin; and how was a man to be explained unless you at least knew somebody who knew his father or mother? . . .
   All cleverness, whether in the rapid use of that difficult instrument the tongue, or in some other art unfamiliar to villagers, was in itself suspicious: honest folks, born and bred in a visible manner, were not overwise or clever – at least not beyond such a matter as knowing the signs of the weather.

Here the narrator is setting the scene for the novel but also establishing the attitude of the villagers to newcomers and her own attitude to the villages themselves. Although she seems genial, she is also critical of their limited outlook and their distrust of anything new. The narrator in this novel has a tight control over the information given to the reader. She is omniscient. The great ladies in their posh clothes have 'toy' spinning wheels. She describes the pallid undersize men as 'aliens' and this is how they are viewed by the inhabitants of the village. She has her tongue in her cheek when she suggests that people whose ancestry is not known should be viewed with the greatest caution.

Part Two of the novel is set sixteen years after the beginning of the story and opens with a group of people leaving a church. The reader is gradually reminded of the main characters and is told how they have aged. The text reads like instructions for a film script with the narrator guiding the camera shots. The narrator is directly addressing the reader here.

Foremost among these advancing groups of well-clad people, there are some whom we shall recognise, in spite of Time, who has laid his hand on them all. The tall blond man of forty is not much changed in feature from the Godfrey Cass of six-and twenty: he is fuller in flesh, and has only lost the indefinable look of youth – a loss which is marked even when the eye is undulled and the wrinkles are not yet come. Perhaps the pretty woman, not much younger than he, who is leaning on his arm, is more changed than her husband: the lovely bloom that used to be always on her cheek now comes but fitfully, with the fresh morning air or with some strong surprise; yet to all who love human faces best for what they tell of human experience, Nancy's beauty has a heightened interest. Often the soul is ripened into fuller goodness while age has spread an ugly film, so that mere glances can never divine the preciousness of the fruit. But the years have not been so cruel to Nancy . . .
    Mr and Mrs Godfrey Cass . . . have turned round to look for the tall, aged gentleman and the plainly dressed woman who are a little behind . . . we will not follow them now; for may there not be some others in this departing congregation whom we should like to see again . . .

The narrator continues to describe characters as they leave the church and gradually reveals who they are. The reader recognises them but is intrigued to find out what has caused the changes – other than the passing of time.

The point of view from which the story is told in *Silas Marner* changes. We see Godfrey Cass's uncertainty and lack of determination. We see the devious thoughts of his brother Dunstan as he contemplates robbery and we see Nancy's thoughts as she awaits her husband's return on one particular fateful afternoon. The beginning of Chapter 18 is a good one to study to show how Eliot narrates the events from a different perspective. It begins:

Some one opened the door at the other end of the room, and Nancy felt it was her husband. She turned from the window with gladness in her eyes, for the wife's chief dread was stilled.

We see the outward appearance of Godfrey as described by Nancy and her mental reaction to his words is given. The reader is in Nancy's mind and experiences her thoughts and feelings.

The novel *The Remains of the Day* by Kazuo Ishiguro is narrated through the eyes of the butler, a persona, who unwittingly witnessed important appeasement negotiations prior to the Second World War. It is therefore a first person narrative with all the implications of that method of storytelling, for example, misinterpretation and self-deception. The story is as much about a journey into the butler's past as it is about the journey he undertakes to visit an old friend. It begins:

It seems increasingly likely that I will undertake the expedition that has been preoccupying my imagination now for some days. An expedition, I should say, which I will undertake alone, in the comfort of Mr Farraday's Ford; an expedition which, as I foresee it, will take me through much of the finest countryside of England to the West country, and may keep me away from Darlington Hall for as much as five or six days.

You may have already read Harper's Lee's novel *To Kill a Mocking Bird* where the events of one summer in the deep South of the United States are related by a child who was part of them.

Multiple narrators

As you realise, stories can be told from a variety of viewpoints. Sometimes it can be told from several viewpoints at the same time. Comparing novels with this structure would be an interesting study. Characters can be talking to you the reader, talking to themselves, or we can be following their train of thought. These different approaches have an effect on the style.

Julian Barnes' novel *Talking It Over* explores the relationship between three people who are talking to the reader. It's almost as if they are addressing a camera or a psychiatrist.

ACTIVITY 69

Here are the first words of each of the three main characters in *Talking It Over*. What can you say about (1) the style in which each is written and (2) what you learn about the personality of each speaker?

All three extracts are in a colloquial style and are meant to imitate the inconsistencies and repetition of speech.

(i)

Stuart. My name is Stuart, and I remember everything. Stuart's my Christian name. My full name is Stuart Hughes. My full name: that's all there is to it. No middle name. Hughes was the name of my parents, who were married for twenty-five years. They called me Stuart. I didn't particularly like the name at first – I got called things like Stew and Stew-Pot at school – but I've got used to it. I can handle it. I can handle my name.

Sorry, I'm not very good at jokes. People have told me that before. Anyway Stuart Hughes – I think that'll do for me. I don't want to be called St John de Vere Knatchbull. My parents were called Hughes. They died, and now I've got their name. And when I die, I'll still be called Stuart Hughes. There aren't many certainties in this great big world of ours, but that's one of them.

(ii)

Gillian. Look I just don't particularly think it's anyone's business. I really don't. I'm an ordinary, private person. I haven't got anything to say. Wherever you turn nowadays there are people who insist on spilling their lives at you. Open any newspaper and they're shouting Come Into My Life. Turn on the television and every second programme has some one talking about his or her problems, his or her divorce, his or her illegitimacy, his or her illness, alcoholism, drug addiction, sexual violation, bankruptcy, cancer, amputation, psychotherapy. His vasectomy, her mastectomy, his or her appendicectomy. What are they all doing it for? Look At Me, Listen To Me. Why can't they simply get on with things? Why do they have to *talk* about it all?

(iii)

Oliver. Hi, I'm Oliver, Oliver Russell. Cigarette? No, I didn't think you would. You don't mind if I do? Yes I *do* know it's bad for my health as a matter of fact, that's why I like it. God, we've only just met and you're coming on like some rampant nut-eater. What's it got to do with you anyway? In fifty years I'll be dead and you'll be a sprightly lizard slurping yoghurt through a straw, sipping peat-bog water and wearing health sandals. Well, I prefer it this way.

Final journeys

ACTIVITY 70

In the novel *As I Lay Dying* by William Faulkner, it is as if the characters are talking to themselves or thinking things over. The novel is the story of the burial journey of the mother of the family. Here is a section from the youngest character's narrative. The style here is almost like stream of consciousness where we are sharing the innermost thoughts of the speaker as they pass from one subject to another. The character is called Vardaman. Dewey Dell, Pa and Cash are names of some of the rest of the family.

When they get it finished they are going to put her in it and then for a long time I couldn't say it. I saw the dark stand up and go whirling away and I said 'Are you going to nail her up in it, Cash? Cash? Cash?' I got shut up in the crib and the new door it was too heavy for me it went shut I couldn't breathe because the rat was breathing up all the air. I said 'Are you going to nail it shut, Cash? Nail it? *Nail* it?'

Pa walks round. His shadow walks around, over Cash going up and down above the saw, at the bleeding plank.

Dewey Dell said we will get some bananas. The train is behind the glass, red on the track. When it runs the track shines on and off. Pa said flour and sugar and coffee costs so much. Because I am a country boy because boys in town. Bicycles. Why do flour and sugar and coffee cost so much when he is a country boy. 'Wouldn't you ruther have some bananas instead?' Bananas are gone, eaten. Gone. When it runs on the track shines again. 'Why ain't I a town boy, pa?' I said God made me. I did not said to God to make me in the country. If he can make a train, why can't he make them all in the town because flour and sugar and coffee. 'Wouldn't you ruther have bananas?'

How do you know Vardaman is upset at his mother's death? What are the main things on his mind in this extract? What do you learn about Pa and Dewey Dell? Explain how his confusion is shown in the text.

Graham Swift's *Last Orders* is another novel with multiple narrators. It is also the tale of a burial journey. In this novel the narrative technique is more traditional 'storytelling' even though chapters are told by different characters. Compare the following extract, which is the opening of *Last Orders,* with previous extracts which are in the first person. You should look at the qualities of speech which are there as well as the register.

If you can get hold of a transcript of speech you will see incredible differences. Real speech is repetitive. It is difficult to divide into sentences. It contains fillers like *er* and *umm*. It is disorganised and often grammatically incorrect. There is hesitation. In fact if you try to *read* a transcript of real speech you will have great difficulty. You will not have any difficulty in reading aloud the following portrayal of real speech.

Bermondsey

It ain't like your regular sort of day.

Bernie pulls me a pint and puts it in front of me. He looks at me puzzled, with his loose, doggy face but he can tell I don't want no chit-chat. That's why I'm here, five minutes after opening, for a little silent pow-wow with a pint glass. He can see the black tie, though it's four days since the funeral. I hand him a fiver and he takes it to the till and brings back my change. He puts the coins, extra gently, eyeing me, on the bar beside the pint.

'Won't be the same, will it?' he says, shaking his head and looking a little way along the bar, like at an unoccupied space. 'Won't be the same.'

I say, 'You ain't seen the last of him yet.'

He says, 'You what?'

I sip the froth off my beer. 'I said you ain't seen the last of him yet.'

He frowns, scratching his cheek, looking at me. 'Course, Ray,' he says and moves off down the bar.

I never meant to make no joke of it.

I suck an inch off my pint and light up a snout. There's maybe three or four other early birds apart from me, and the place don't look at its best. Chilly, a whiff of disinfectant, too much empty space. There's a shaft of sunlight coming through the window full of specks. Makes you think of a church.

Flashbacks

In *The Playmaker* the first sentence is:

He began hearing for the parts in the play early in April, the day after the hanging of Private Handy Baker and the five other Marines.

The ghost of Handy Baker haunts one of the characters and the hanging of the marines is a thread that runs through the text, but it is not until Chapter 25 that the reader understands why. This is when the explanation is given and this is when the jigsaw becomes complete. The whole book contains a series of flashbacks about the background of the characters and their lives before they arrived and founded Sydney. We watch and read as something happens and the explanation is given much later. Gradually the jigsaw fits together much to our satisfaction.

In *Silas Marner* by George Eliot we see the main character, a recluse who shies away from any social contact with other villagers, at his loom weaving. Within a few pages we are transported to fifteen years earlier and the background of Silas explains his behaviour. This secret is shared with the reader. In the rest of the book most of the secrets of the story are shared with the reader. All we have to do is await the revelation to the characters.

ACTIVITY 72

Using a text you know well, see if it is written chronologically. If it is, rearrange the story briefly so that there are flashbacks and see what effect this has.

If flashbacks are used, re-arrange the story briefly in chronological order. You can do this in the form of a time line. Start at the edge of the page with the earliest incident that is referred to and mark points as you get to them in the text. A worked example of this can be found on p. 30 of *Living Literature*. The time line is for the play *Cat on a Hot Tin Roof* but the method is the same.

In this chapter you have been reminded of some of the technical words you need to use when you are describing the style of a text and shown how to use them. We have also looked at the point of view from which the text is narrated and two specific structural techniques; multiple narrators and flashbacks which add an intriguing dimension to some texts.

And finally

Comparing texts is fascinating but it does take some work and not a little organisation. You should try to use some of the techniques suggested here to provide evidence for your comments and coherence to your arguments. Many possible texts to compare have been suggested in this book and you have probably already come up with many more. Although you must adhere to the subject specifications, hopefully you will be able to choose to link texts which you enjoy and which allow you to show your knowledge and skill as well as your interest.

Appendix

Frogs and Christmas!

The essay below was written by a student. The task left the choice of poems completely to the student and gave little guidance about what was expected, except that the response should be no longer than about 1,000 words. A tall order! However, a very creditable answer was produced. The student chose two poems which she particularly liked – always a good starting point!

ACTIVITY 73

This book has looked at linking texts through a variety of aspects: genre, theme, cultural connections, style and structure. Read the essay carefully and see if this essay tackles the comparison through these perspectives and give your evidence. The student did not actually have the advantage of reading this book! The two poems are reprinted below. Study them first.

Death of a Naturalist

All year the flax-dam festered in the heart
Of the townland; green and heavy headed
Flax had rotted there, weighted down by huge sods.
Daily it sweltered in the punishing sun.
Bubbles gargled delicately, bluebottles
Wove a strong gauze of sound around the smell.
There were dragon-flies, spotted butterflies,
But best of all was the warm thick slobber
Of frogs spawn that grew like clotted water
In the shade of the banks. Here, every spring
I would fill jampotfuls of the jellied
Specks to range on window-sills at home,
On shelves at school, and wait and watch until
The fattening dots burst into nimble-
Swimming tadpoles. Miss Walls would tell us how
The daddy frog was called a bullfrog
And how he croaked and how the mammy frog
Laid hundreds of little eggs and this was
Frogspawn. You could tell the weather by frogs too
For they were yellow in the sun and brown
In rain

Then one hot day when the fields were rank
With cowdung in the grass the angry frogs
Invaded the flax-dam; I ducked through hedges
To a coarse croaking that I had not heard
Before. The air was thick with a bass chorus.
Right down the dam gross bellied frogs were cocked
On sods; their loose necks pulsed like sails. Some hopped:
The slap and plop were obscene threats. Some sat
Poised like mud grenades, their blunt heads farting.
I sickened, turned and ran. The great slime kings
Were gathered there for vengeance and I knew
That if I dipped my hand the spawn would clutch it.

Seamus Heaney

Christmas Shopping

Spending beyond their income on gifts for Christmas –
Swing doors and crowded lifts and draperied jungles –
What shall we buy for our husbands and sons
Different from last year?

Foxes hang by their noses behind plate glass –
Scream of macaws across festoons of paper –
Only the faces on the boxes of chocolates are free
From boredom and crowsfeet.

Sometimes a chocolate box-girl escapes in the flesh,
Lightly manoeuvres the crowd, trilling with laughter;
After a couple of years her feet and brain will
Tire like the others.

The great windows marshal their troops for assault on the purse
Something and eleven a yard, hoodwinking logic,
The eleventh hour draining the gurgling pennies
Down to the conduits

Down to the sewers of money-rats and marshgas –
Bubbling in the maundering music under the pavement;
Here go the hours of routine, the weight on our eyelids –
Pennies on corpses'.

While over the street in the centrally heated public
Library dwindling figures with sloping shoulders
And hands in pockets, weighted down in the boots like chessmen,
Stare at the printed

Columns of ads, the quickset road to riches,
Starting at a little and temporary but once we're
Started who knows whether we shan't continue
Salaries rising,

Rising like salon against the bullnecked river,
Bound for the spawning ground of carefree days –
Good for a fling before the golden wheels run
Down to a standstill.

And Christ is born – The nursery glad with baubles,
Alive with light and washable paint and children's
Eyes, expects as its due the accidental
Loot of system.

Smell of the south – oranges in silver paper,

Dates with ginger, the benison of firelight,
The blue flames dancing round the brandied raisins,
Smiles from above them,

Hands from above them as of gods but really
These their parents, always seen from below, them-
Selves are always anxious looking across the
Fence to the future –

Out there lies the future gathering quickly
Its blank momentum; through the tubes of London
The dead winds blow the crowds like beasts in flight from
Fire in the forest.

The little firtrees palpitate with candles
In hundreds of clattering households where the suburb
Straggles like nervous handwriting, the margin
Blotted with smokestacks.

Further out on the coast the light house moves its
Arms of light through the fog that wads our welfare,
Moves its arms like a giant at Swedish drill whose
Mind is a vacuum.

Louis MacNeice

Here is the student's essay.

COMPARE AND CONTRAST TWO SHORT POEMS

I have chosen for this essay *Death of a Naturalist* by Seamus Heaney and *Christmas Shopping* by Louis MacNeice. The common theme is disillusionment: in *Death of a Naturalist* the sudden disillusionment of a child; in *Christmas Shopping* the considered disillusionment of an adult.

The poems are comparable in that both poets use free verse and both rely heavily on enjambment, or run-on lines, to maintain the flow of the narrative: Heaney's
    All year the flax-dam festered in the heart
    Of the townland . . .
and MacNeice's
    After a couple of years her feet and her brain will
    Tire like the others.
Both also very effectively use imagery to evoke the reader's senses. Heaney's
'Bubbles gargled delicately' and
    bluebottles
    Wove a <u>s</u>trong gauze of <u>s</u>ound around the <u>s</u>mell,
with its sibilant alliteration to deepen the sensory appeal, for me conjures up a vivid impression of rank decay. MacNeice's
    The eleventh hour draining the gurgling pennies
    <u>Down</u> the conduits
    <u>Down</u> to the sewers of money –
summons up similar unpleasant sensations, although in this case anadiplosis, or repetition, is used to give added depth to the waste product (money).

The poets are otherwise quite different in their styles. *Death of a Naturalist* is a narrative, written in the first person. The tone is warm and sensual, the atmosphere sleepy, becoming nightmarish. The first two lines set the scene with the alliteration '<u>f</u>lax-dam <u>f</u>estered' to conjure up a picture and smell of rottenness, reinforced by being daily 'sweltered in the punishing sun'. There is a strong semantic field throughout the first verse and into the second, to establish this rottenness: 'festered', 'rotted', 'bubbles gurgled delicately', 'clotted water', 'rank'. The memory of the child's eagerness to collect the 'jellied Specks', as he calls the frogspawn, is so vivid to the adult narrator that he reverts for a time to childish language: 'Miss Walls would tell us how the daddy frog' . . . and Irish dialect, 'mammy frog'. He returns to adult language in the second verse when recalling the horror of seeing the frogs gathered for mating. He is convinced they are there to exact their revenge on him for all the stolen frogspawn. To reinforce this tone of menace, Heaney introduces a second semantic field, this time of war: 'invaded', 'cocked', 'threats', 'grenades', 'vengeance'. The narrator's memory of his sense of disgust is vivid: 'rank with cowdung', '<u>c</u>oarse' '<u>c</u>roaking' (alliteration and onomatopoeia to double the harsh sound). The onomatopoeic consonance 'slap and slop' conveys his disgust and horror at the fat bodies waiting 'poised like hand grenades'. The child's terror and fear that the metaphorical 'great slime kings' (which sounds much more horrific than 'frogs') were there for vengeance and that the spawn would this time clutch his hand, give this poem a nightmarish ending.

In contrast, *Christmas Shopping* is mainly cold and flat in tone. It is a social comment written by a critical onlooker, saddened by people's willingness to continue with a wasteful tradition whilst others do not even have a job. I think it is important to bear in mind that the poem was written in the 1930s, as MacNeice uses archaic terms, e.g. 'Swedish drill', and the allusion in the twelfth verse to the forthcoming World War II would otherwise have no meaning. The opening theme is of wastefulness and how people continue to be beguiled into 'Spending beyond their incomes for Christmas' by the 'hoodwinking logic' of 'Something-and-eleven the yard' (archaic language and equivalent to today's £1.99 a metre sounding cheaper than £2 a metre). MacNeice likens the shops to 'draperied jungles', a metaphor which is reinforced by the 'Scream of macaws across festoons of paper', very powerful imagery which jars the senses. He has personified 'the eleventh hour' (or last minute) to make it appear as though it has tricked the shoppers and is now 'draining the gurgling pennies/Down the conduits' and so into the sewers of money. The money bubbles 'in <u>m</u>aundering <u>m</u>usic under the pavement', a pleasant-sounding alliteration but really a bitter description of the rambling, pointless waste whilst over the street the unemployed keep warm in the public library. The unemployed are described as 'dwindling figures with <u>s</u>loping <u>s</u>houlders' – a metaphor which evokes a picture of dejection and hopelessness, reinforced by the alliteration. 'Weighted in the boots like chessmen' – a good simile meaning that they have no more animation left than a chess piece, or perhaps to show they are merely political pawns. The tone then lightens briefly with the brightly lit nursery 'glad with baubles', i.e. brightly decorated. (Even here MacNeice cannot avoid a cynical note, describing the Christmas presents and food the children can expect as the 'accidental/Loot of a system'.) The lighter tone continues with

<u>S</u>mell of the <u>S</u>outh – oranges in silver paper,
Dates and ginger

(the alliteration strengthening the exotic feel of the verse) and 'benison (blessing) of firelight' – a suggestion of warmth in an otherwise chilly poem. Their parents present them with smiling faces but are

always anxious looking across the
Fence to the future –
Out there lies the future gathering quickly/Its blank momentum" –

surely a reference to the fear of the future World War II, approaching with increasing but unknown speed. There is a military semantic field in the final verse: '<u>A</u>rms of light', '<u>w</u>ads our welfare' and 'Swedish <u>drill</u>'. ('Swedish drill' was a form of PE taught in schools in the earlier part of the twentieth century, the arm movements echoing the 'Arms of light' from a lighthouse).

I like these two poems equally but for very different reasons. *Death of a Naturalist* because of its rich, figurative language and vivid imagery, *Christmas Shopping* because of its thought provoking and rather haunting qualities. I will never again view frogs or Christmas in quite the same way!

COMMENTARY The student begins with a clear statement of the chosen poems and the main reason she linked them. She chose them because to her they had a common theme of disillusion. She then goes on to show how there is a variation of this theme – 'sudden disillusionment of a child' and the 'considered disillusionment of an adult'. If there is a weakness in this response it is the rather brief reference to this theme which would have benefited from more development.

Paragraph two continues the comparison looking at the similarities in form and style (use of sensuous imagery). At least one of the words she uses will have you rushing to a dictionary! She comments on the effect of the features she has spotted.

Paragraphs three and four offer a comprehensive stylistic analysis of both the poems looking in detail at imagery, semantic fields and tone. The student demonstrates a good knowledge of technical terms and poetic techniques.

The final paragraph gives a nice personal response which shows the student's engagement with the texts.

Although there is some reference to the cultural background of the texts this could have been developed. The poets are both Irish with the MacNeice poem probably being written thirty years before the Heaney. Cultural/historical issues are mentioned briefly in the essay – the Irish dialect and the imminent war in Europe.

This is a creditable essay by a very good student. She chose challenging texts which may not have been chosen as subject matter by a less talented and less methodical student. If there are weaknesses they are the result of the lack of guidance in the question itself and the restrictive word count.

Perhaps you will be able to link 'frogs' and 'Christmas' from now on!